ESSENTIAL
ASTONISHMENTS

poetic reflections for awakening

Gina Mazza

with

Scott A. Terrell | Donna Knutson | Atul Ranchod
Meredith Lowry | Gershon Mitchel

Also by Gina Mazza

Everything Matters, Nothing Matters:
For Women Who Dare to Live
with Exquisite Calm, Euphoric Creativity
and Divine Clarity
St. Lynn's Press

Romancing the Future
(with Judy Julin)
Findhorn Press

The Highest and The Best:
A Gifted Healer's Vision of
Third-Millennium Medicine and
Humanity's Intuitive Evolution
(with Sallie Christensen)
Xlibris Corp.

To Frances,
for giving me courage
by recognizing
what I had.

MID MARCH - 2024

ERICA -
    A BIT of insight to one
of your patients + I'm the
last poet on this Book -
good luck at your new gig -

        gershon
        AKA - NAPKiN Dignity the
            EXPOUNDER

Contents

POEMS BY SCOTT A. TERRELL

POEMS BY DONNA KNUTSON

POEMS BY ATUL RANCHOD

POEMS BY GERSHON MITCHEL

POEMS BY GINA MAZZA

"We shall not cease from exploration
And the end of all our exploring
Will be to arrive where we started
And know the place for the first time."

—T. S. Elliot

God

I Did It All for Love

"It is my hope that you will like
this creation that I've created,"
God must have said,
"and that one day,
you will understand my motivation.

I did it all for Love.

That is why any hate revolution
leads nowhere but
in the wrong direction.

It defies my intention—

and that disappoints Me more
than anything else
even I can imagine."

—Gina Mazza

The Only Religion Worth Fighting For

Love is the only religion worth fighting for.

No faith that speaks to separation
comes from Me.
Give up bickering
like school children on recess.

Time is running out—
at least, the kind of time
you care about so passionately.
If your worship of time was pure,
you would not squander it.

Fireflies burn bright and die quickly.
This is how you should live—

like tiny lanterns winging around
illuminating the dark,
not trying to conquer it.

For what shall it profit a man
if he gains the whole world
yet loses his soul?

—Gina Mazza

Stop Being So Human

War only echoes incoherence.
Why sound the alarm of separateness
when I have given you the keys to the Kingdom?

Next to nothing is yours.
These are not possessions.
It is all a gift.
Cherish and share freely.
Be astounded by My abundance,
not selfish of it.

How can I say this?
Stop being so human!

Right now, start being that part of you
that is eternal.
Right now, open the gate inside
where grace thrives.
Remember your immortality?

The way to greatness does not
lie on the killing field.
Only a fool would shoot off his own leg
for a dollar, yet
you do this to My utopia.

Seek higher, beyond illusion;

beyond being human.
You were designed for potential
that far exceeds this shallow play.

Grow up to your capacity.
Exit the sandbox.
You are adults now in this new age.

Drink the fine wine of truth.
Become drunk, even, on it.
Allow it to shatter your inhibitions.

Set aside puppetry; that is for children.
If you can split the atom,
you can save lives
from your own treachery.

Read the colors of the rainbow as a scripture
and write a new story.
Deliverance is up for grabs
by those who see brightest.

Turn on your inner lamp and light the way—
the only true sustainable energy.
It can move mountains.

Create missives, not missiles.
One is magic;
the other, tragic.
That story is badly tattered, like
the hem of an outworn coat.

Take it off, finally.

Once in ecstasy,
there is no need for this nonsense.

—Gina Mazza

Pray Only for This

Awaken, my friends.

Pray only for this:
To see the face of God
with #nofilter and no falsity.

This is the only obsession
that comes to any good.

If you want to be famous,
be so for sharing this truth alone.

Lay down all arms and pick up alms.

Sway them
to create a breeze of compassion
rippling through every
beating heart.

—Gina Mazza

Speak Only of Splendor

All of life is a plenteous wonderland.
Few see this for what it is.

By now, you shouldn't be surprised.
My glory is boundless.
Just look around.

Blowfish mimic My intelligence.
Every grass blade is silent witness
to My wind song.
Notice that the dove flies high
and rock melts deep in My core.

It's a panoply of sensations
just for you, My love.

Behold in your heart an appreciation
for every living thing.
That is the way of saints and sages,
both of which you are.

Complaining is a waste dump
with no exit; a trap,
a mind cage.

Speak only of splendor.

—Gina Mazza

Next Exegesis

Prepare to reinvent *everything*.
YOUR occasion to create has arrived,
the unseen soon apparent.

Be as I AM,
all Great Wisdom in One.
You are same, a fractal
of the Master's palette.

Things you could never imagine,
I have. It is done.
Now . . . make it *real*-ity.
Shatter all patterns.
Let the scraps fly and recontextualize.
You know how.
If not this moment, you will.

Nothing is static inside Divine providence.
Oscillation, vibration.
This spiral of change, a constant gift of life—
new worlds born inside the body
and cosmos every second.

Slip into the mind of an imaginal cell.
Stay present and listen.
Greatness is at hand.

Now grab a pen / brush / hammer
and get started.

—Gina Mazza

Everything

Once upon a day,
there was nothing
and then everything,
including days.

This is My gift,
which I am gifting
to My own creation,
including you.

Now rest
and remember:

I put everything
into the hands
of those
who put everything
in My hands.

—Gina Mazza

Tear Gas

I tell you:

No one,
absolutely
no one

is free
is safe
so long as hatred
is in hearts
and
self-centricism
is on minds.

No measure of
firearms,
militia,
policy,
censorship,
borders,
bank in bank,
gerrymandering,
demagoguery,
or guard dogs at the top

will save you.

Indulge this fantasy
at your own peril.
Or wake up!
Strip off your grave clothes
and walk out!

Only you have medicine to cure
your temporal blindness.

Cease clinging in quiet desperation
to what is yours
and what is theirs.

Humanity is in this together.
Get that or all else fails.
ALL
of
it.

—Gina Mazza

Love

Habituate Compassion

Keep choosing love until it is rote.
Habituate compassion.

Be a rebel that way.

The most gangster thing you can do
is forgive and begin again.

Every day,
one step in a positive direction
is two paces away from Armageddon.

Let the sun set on the old ways.

By now, we are more than primates.
Stop acting so primitive.
The future, if we have one,
is a shimmering footpath
to our star destiny.

Guarantees are not guaranteed.
Proceed as if you have none.

Re-create the probability
that life will continue
instead of the inevitability
that it will desist.

That, my friend,
is true power—

a superpower
that will end all war
and annihilate its necessity.

—Gina Mazza

Love is Not Scarier Than Hatred

Every new dawn is calling you to choose differently.
Listen! Awaken with ears to hear.
Engage your personal sonar,
your echolocation.

Hear the new apologue yearning to be written.
Be the scribe.
Just take dictation.
Do not judge.

We are creatures made for creation,
not destruction.
Though once savages, we have graduated.
You can't give back the diploma
or renounce the learning.
One cannot un-know
what history has wrought.

Stand at the cliff's edge
and trust the free fall.
After all,
love is not scarier than hatred.

Study the habits of symbiosis.

Look through the microscope of beauty
and see the oneness of this world—

it's true nature,
and the nature of truth—
the only thing that's real.

For those who are still desperate for sleep
will be overcome by it.

—Gina Mazza

Our Only Option

Ironic
that Love has become
our only option,
the only way we can
continue to survive
despite loud opinions
to the contrary.

Sound bites fixate on what is wrong.
It's time for the brass section
to step up
and trumpet

what is good
what is just
what is prudent
what is consequential
what is inspiring
what is courageous.

Become poets of the sublime.

It can't hurt nearly as much
as the murder that is
so pervasive on our planet.

—Gina Mazza

Reverence is More Powerful Than Atomic Weapons

But how do I do this, you ask?
It is illusive,
slippery to grasp the big picture
in the clamor of everyday life.

I say to you:
Nothing that's driven your species forward
happened overnight.
Slow, subtle increments of growth,
unrelenting,
are what causes the organism
to transcend into something
beyond what it was.

Just reorient your goal
from one of greed
to one of gratitude.
It's really that simple, as a first step.

Stand back and assess where greed has gotten you.
Better yet, imagine where gratitude can get you.

Reverence is more powerful
than atomic weapons.
You just haven't learned this yet.

Higher education awaits.
Enter the university of the soul.
Become shrewd as a mystic
who penetrates all bullshit.

This emerging story is magical.
If I were you, I'd be excited.

—Gina Mazza

Going Viral

[written the year before the Covid-19 pandemic]

What if the Great Plague
had a spontaneous relapse,
a second coming?

This time,
a pandemic of benevolence.

What brings on
our black death
is this contagion of hate,
of wishing ill—not good—will.

It's time to go viral
with tenderness and mercy
in all the right places
throughout this worldwide
web of humanity.

May we all fall sick with Love for one another.

Inoculable and unable to walk
unless it's
towards the light—

unable to speak
unless with high tolerance.

Caring cures.
Develop a fever for it.

—Gina Mazza

Imagine

LOVE, our religion.
WISDOM, our compass.
NATURE, our sacred temple.
WORDS, our spoken prayers.

ANIMALS, our friends.
MUSIC, our emotion.
RAIN, our holy water.
KINDNESS, our practice.

HOPE, our salvation.
GRACE, our redemption.
PAIN, our medicine.
ART, our joy.

SUN, our warmth.
SON, our Way-Truth-Life.

Can you see it?

We've got everything
we've ever longed for.

—Gina Mazza

Life

Life is Not Ambition

#1

Life is not ambition.
That is for fools who don't know
what's really going on here.
I once was one of them.
I assumed the position.
Didn't think twice about it—
too busy reaching and climbing.
The precipice was somewhat prescribed;
all I had to do was make it there,
then I will have made it,
or have it made,
or so I was taught.

Quarter-way through, it came clear:
This is the wrong ladder—the way up
based on a map charted long before
I knew myself.
Yes, I could have made it,
would have made it—
did make it, to some degree,
though curious:
What's the "it" I'm making?

Descending would mean death
and the voices are so insistent,

shoving you upward, saying:
don't forsake what you've got!
show some appreciation!
suck it up!
get out of the way or prepare
to be trampled!

So, I prayed for a parachute, and it appeared.
Deftly, I sprung from the rung
and landed on a mountaintop,
where the view is unobstructed.

Now I can breathe.
Now I can see the entire landscape.
It's quiet enough here to hear
my inner voice, and those of my ancestors,
beseeching me to do the thing
they couldn't do.

I'm never coming down from this mountain.
It's my home now,
above the chatter of low places
and bodies, busier than ants,
toiling in un-unison.

#2

Ambition is a slippery slope.
Climb too high
and your head's in the clouds.
Where you came from is no longer visible.
True north is obscured.

You find yourself in a fog,
not instrument rated.
This is what happens—
you lose sight of the horizon
and become disoriented.
You confuse
up with down,
east with west.
You shoulder on, though, hoping that
once you reach the next milestone
or break through that glass ceiling,
the skies will open
and the Hallelujah chorus will commence.

Instead, you realize
there's no room at the top
for elation, because now
it's
all
down
hill.

Join me over here,
where the ground is firm
and the natural order of things
inspires the hike.
There's room enough for
a celebration of thousands,
for stargazing,
and daydreaming,
and toasted marshmallows on willow twigs.

We can pitch tents under the tree canopy,
kindle a holy fire and share stories
of our own vast uniqueness.
We could even give awards,
like the good scouts we are,
to those whose chosen paths
were most untrodden—
and praise how we raised each other up
when waters raged high
and footing proved treacherous.

At this exalted altitude,
no one serves platitudes like:
"Hey, why did you wander off like that?"
"How stupid for not staying with the tried and true."
"Imitation is the sincerest form of flattery"—
as if flattery is a virtue.
"You could have gotten seriously hurt, or lost."

Let's be serious, then.
Blindly following the known path guarantees
nothing, and I'd rather
exquisitely fall to my death—
as only I can—
than lose my soul
to someone else's banal notion
of what really matters
at the end of life's hike.

—Gina Mazza

Life is Not That Special

Life is not that special.
If you believe this, are you an ingrate?
Look around.
We act as if this is the case.

The signs are everywhere; I need not repeat them here.
Suffice to say that we bring ruination
to people and planet.
We toil under the corrosive belief that
both are expendable,
undeserving,
inferior,
replaceable.

So let's just call ourselves on it:
Life is not that special.
If we would actually adopt this belief
that we are acting out,
if we admit to it, what would happen?

I can sit here and say the rooster crowing
across the road is maddening,
the farmer letting cows out to pasture is ordinary,
the rosebuds and zinnias bursting forth in the garden
are nearly worth noticing because there will be
plenty more blooms next week or next year.

But will there be roosters and cows
and rosebuds and gardens
in our future at the rate we're going?
Is this the ultimate case of
"you don't know what you've got 'til it's gone?"

Okay, let's just call ourselves on it:
Life is not that special.
Let's just save ourselves all the suffering
and get on with our demise.
It's our choice:
We can act as if everything is precious
or nothing is precious.

We've become numb to the sanctity of life
in all its forms.
We don't get the difference between
dominion and dominance.

Well let's just call ourselves on it:
Life is not that special.
Let's just turn back into ash, into hardened rock,
into single cells that don't give a damn,
into vapor that dissipates
into the cosmic atmosphere.

How callous, you might think.
What about my children?
My grandchildren? My great-grandchildren?
That's the point here.
What future are we leaving them?
Will there even be a world for them

to be born into?

Oh wait . . . Now you care?
Now that it's personal?
Well then, you might want to edit your position.
Maybe life is special after all, you say?

What would you give for it?
Would you change your insular ways?
Would you do what's necessary
to thrive or even survive?
Do you understand?

—Gina Mazza

What's This Ride For?

Life is a carousel.
Sometimes up,
sometimes down.

Always turning,
slowly, towards
an unknown end.

Winged ponies. Wooden unicorns.
Lights and mirrors.
Dazed and dizzying.

Einstein once said:
"The eternal mystery of the world
is its comprehensibility."
We stagger towards understanding.

Meanwhile, the organ waltzes
as we clutch the brass ring,
vying for a free go-round.

What's this ride for,
if not amusement?

—Gina Mazza

Heaven on Earth

We are here
to be of service—
not servitude—
to one another.

Should you see a means
to make this world better,
begin.

It's not a distraction
from your real life.

It *is* real life,

and at this mature hour,
honestly,
anything less than Heaven on Earth
is beneath us.

—Gina Mazza

Inwardness

An Arrival of Virtuosity

[For Cheryl]

There is plenty to concern myself with today.
For now, I open the window sash
and catch sight of the quarter moon
beyond the tree line.
Soon the lavender sky
will recede and
light will break
as it does, faithfully,
every day.

Lucid miracles like these
are here for taking unto yourself,
like a psalm inscribed
in some unnamed place.

Should I turn on Deva and Miten,
or should I sit unadorned by sound?
Today I choose to chant
the mantra of my soul,
my own heart sutra.

This is what poets do:
They sit and listen
for what feels pure and true
in a bursting instant.

It's not a convergence
of thoughts; but rather,
an arrival of virtuosity
conducted straight from
the heart of God.

Play me, Lord,
like a finely tuned instrument
in your orchestra.
I cannot read music
but help me keep my pitch
on perfect You.

—Gina Mazza

Illumination

Wild thoughts flow recklessly
through my head
in a fluster of surrender.

I stop midstream and observe
the inner view.

Drip
by
drip
by
drip
by
drip
the Light seeps into my system.

I sit, illumined.

Is this Rumi
streaming through me,
or my own heart wisdom?

No matter.
I embrace the radiance,
learning more about

this thing
called

Life—
and my place in it.

—Gina Mazza

No Wonder We're Angry

I like to wake early
and tease the sun awake.
The birds join my ritual,
sometimes a few tree frogs.

Not much happening in these early hours.
Yet everything is happening.
Nature rests, but never sleeps.

Humans sleep, but never seem to rest.
No wonder we're angry!
Where is the reprieve?
Where is the sweet letting go of all worry?
Who makes time for that?

I rise early to make time for that.
I stretch and feel my human form.
If nothing hurts, I give thanks.
If something hurts, I vow to seek its cause.
My first thought is of
my children, my love, and other dear ones.

My second thought: coffee.
That, too, is a sacred ritual
brewing my senses alive.
Beans grown on tropical plants and roasted—
who devised that thousands of years ago?

And the Italian ingenuity
that spews forth this nectar—
At five o'clock,
I venerate this innovation,
turning water
into morning wine
in fifteen
seconds
flat.

—Gina Mazza

Now

Yesterdays have lapsed.
The future, a dim vista.
Now.

Now
is that inestimable blip
of undying timelessness.

Only now is where I exist,
never to be again,
and again,
yet again.

Now.
A capricious foray
into everything,
a perpetual seed
readying itself
as mighty redwood.

When I really want to
lavish the
suchness of all,
I place my ardor on
the center of
the moment

then
leave it completely.

All edges implode
then reverse-blast like
a supernova.

The world surmises itself
as I watch, whimsically,
through mine/mind's eye.

The eternal now,
and then some.

—Gina Mazza

Morning Glory

Morning glory,
to what do you ascribe
your blooming?

Born of the dawn,
then done by mid-day,
how precious would
our hours be
if we lived as you do—

bursting color briefly
then twisting final
on the vine by dusk?

Oh, the glory of this wisp
of a chance to breathe into
this other world—
the same one that animates your
inward sensing of the sun!

Inspire us to give praise
to each morning—
for if not glory-full and
etched with gladness in our hearts,
of what use is our own
sacred blossoming?

—Gina Mazza

Incandescent Dreams

In this incredible hour of living,
seconds pass as unconstrued
colors of a prism,
each splayed across an endless
awning of pure potential—
ever becoming, always existing.

If one is wise, waste not
these incandescent dreams of reality.
To squander the breath is death
of a thousand cuts.

Look up and ravish the
sun-drenched sky while you can.
All comes to an end—
even amidst generous perpetual beginnings.

Glide forward through every dusk and dawn
in quiet appreciation—
always giving thanks to the
One Who Forever Was,
Is and
Will Be.

—Gina Mazza

Awakening

Out of the Woods

We are not out of the woods yet.
What the heaven does that mean?

Have we sacrificed at the altar
of pride and avarice so long that
we've lost all direction?

Forgotten
how to read the sun, sense the wind?
what side moss grows on?
the pulse of tree-chatter under soil
and crow's warning from above?
Does the stream still make us weep
or have we extorted all substance
for illegal tender?

Has our trail of breadcrumbs and bloodshed
tricked us too deep into the forest and
obscured many into oblivion?

Bear or wolf or raccoon might say:
"Treading amidst the rubble,
toiling along that rocky path
is a wise existence
but it's not Life itself.

Wake up, humans! You are
so much more than your suffering."

How long can we survive the wild,
alone to each other,
with no pocket knives
or prayers of contrition?

Let us pray then
for enough of a clearing
to see the light,
to exhale a unified sigh
from the soles of our aching feet—
to honor, even in continued nightfall,
our pure north star.

May we relearn
that compass
and compassion
are one and the same—
both lead us home
to our divinity.

—Gina Mazza

Is Karma Real?

Is karma real?
Do we reap what we sow?
I want to know now—
not wait until some future
that may be only mythical.

Cosmic law says we attract what we emit.
Jesus spoke:
"Do unto others as you would
have them do unto you."
Physics asserts that like particles attract like.

But I'm not naïve.
Justice is not always served.
Some seem to get away with murder.
Does it come back around as
a killing of the self?

What if karma was instant,
if we swiftly knew our reverb?
Could we preempt what's coming to us?
Would we do the same deeds?

Or is even knowing that not a deterrent?
The news is filled these days with mass shootings.
The gunman knows his fate and
claims it quite willfully,
surely knowing what lies ahead,
obstinate nonetheless.

It's like there's no punishment
substantial enough to overcome
the woundedness being acted out.

Yet I'm being one-sided here.
Let's talk about the mirror-back of loving deeds.
Do nice guys and good girls finish first?
Not to say it's a competition, but
do more pleasing things happen
in response to acts of compassion?

That's been my experience
but I'm not taking my own word for it.
Let's ask others who routinely pay it forward,
who choose to spread joy like sweet jam
on the bread of existence.

I'll have to get back to you on this,
but my guess is that
they're more likely to lead this world—
and leave it—
with resolution and absolution,
and their time here,
a richer, sweeter ride
to the finish line.

So if we want to call it a human race,
my wager is on those who
run towards kindness,
not cataclysm.

Either way, I presume, karma wins.

—Gina Mazza

Beyond Duality

Hooded specters process through my head.
Life's not always a cakewalk on the inside.
Trauma is a stain not easily scrubbed away.
I'm being honest here.
Things happen that aren't pretty.

Here's where the meaning of life really gets tested.
Deep trouble makes you wonder:
Why am I here? WTF? Why must this happen?

Some offer trite answers:
It's for your own good.
It's a lesson.
Or most dismaying:
You've caused your own suffering.

Is it possible to wake up
from this dream of duality?
Can we do evolution
without emotional wounding?
It seems to set us back.

Seeing contrast is a smart curriculum.
I'm just inquiring:
Why does it have to hurt so bad?
Can we invent a mechanism to ascend
without the crushing weight
of pain and misery?

For starters, let's be better to each other.
Now that we understand
the power of the dark night,
having to endure it becomes redundant,
does it not?

—Gina Mazza

Metamorphosis

Something
opened my wings
as I slept.

Now
I taste nectar
everywhere.

—Gina Mazza

Risk Being Torn to Pieces

If the truth is too bright,
turn your back to the sun.
Let it cast your shadow self
so you can face it,
not run from it.

You can't, anyway.
It will follow you everywhere.

Trust yourself on this:
Faith forward and look
with a heart to see.
No one need watch.
Just walk on.

Go into the cavern you most fear
about yourself
and greet the lion.

Risk being torn to pieces.
It's going to be okay.

—Gina Mazza

Sweet Drowning

I awake from the dream
impelled to take
all the small talk
of claiming sovereignty
of standing in personal power
of being a cosmic force
of having any importance at all
and shove it aside.

Burn it all down to the
pile of rubble that is it.

There is no me.
I am dissolved,
granules of sugar in hot tea,
swallowed whole by the
only One That Ever Is.
This is the price paid.
The cost of devotion:
my own disappearance
into a vast ocean of stillness—

slowly, slowly downward
drowning all desires.
They are no more.
There is no I

to want for,
nothing to long for.
Only a deeper immersion.

Is this how it is now?
No shore to reach?
No breath to catch?
Or is it some brief passage
to a new way of landing?
My body is still here,
after all.

This drowning
is so sweet
it scares me.
Okay then, at least
I can still feel.

My new normal:
drowning in feeling
and feeling the drowning
all at once
as I plead:

Purify me for Your will alone;
I am poised for Thy will to be done.

—Gina Mazza

Truth

How does one come to the Truth?

First, ask. Don't assume.
There is nobility
in not knowing.

Offer respect to the awe.
Deference is requirement one.

All else is a falling into
the feeling
of it.

—Gina Mazza

The Corporeality of Consciousness

I was initiated
into the Real
by way-show-ers
who taught me
life is not
what's on the surface.

The egg cracked open
to expose true substance,
the corporeality of consciousness
that gives rise to form.

I have never been the same since.
Thank Goddess.

Now every moment is a prayer,
all work a contemplative practice,
every face, my mirror.

It helps to have tour guides
familiar with this inner terrain.
It can get treacherous—
deadly, even—
slaying restrictive
behaviors and beliefs.

What remains in the embers of the journey
is the clear white flame of longing,
burning ever bright
for the Beloved.

—Gina Mazza

Step Out of Hiding

Step out of hiding
so God can find you.
Call off the mind beasts.
Tell them to scavenge for
carrion elsewhere
because now you are
hungry for consecration
from the only Source
who can grant it.

Enter the dusty cupboard
of your suppressed fears and shame
before the shelves crack loose.
Swing wide the doors and acknowledge—
the first step towards their dispersion.

How much longer can you live this way?
Mean-spirited
Self-serving
Insatiable
Aching
Empty

Satan is a great metaphor
for someone who cannot see clearly.

For what are you waiting?

Break free of yourself
and repose in the Light.

—Gina Mazza

What Do You Want?

None of this is actually a
moral,
ethical,
theological issue—
keep God and virtue out of it
for just a second.

It's straight sense:
What do you want?

*

Now let's go there,
all you who claim fidelity to a savior:

This is the day the Lord has made.
Rejoice and be glad.
Unceasingly.

Or not—

Curse your breath.
Forget the sun rises for you.
Find every reason to remonstrate.
Extinct whole species.
Blame then cancel the self-perceived enemy.
Take everything for granted.

Keep believing
nothing is sacred,
nowhere is safe.
Continue to beat the drum
of what you don't want.
It's all just discordant noise,
a distraction
from answering:

What do you want?
What do you really, really want?

—Gina Mazza

Get Up and Write!

Thunderous skies
implore me at dawn:

"Get up and write!
Speak of sublimity
through your every
rumbling pore."

From wisps of sleep
my eyes awaken,
startled, as every morning,
by this dream voyage.

Breath alone is miracle.
I follow it, and wait
for that rush
of rain in my veins.

I give my fervor to
the wind's soliloquy,
some to the trees' sway,
and more to the horse's neigh
in neighboring fields.

The Creator I praise
lives in all of it—

wind, tree, horse;
eyes, dreams, breath, veins,

and these words.

—Gina Mazza

I Have Become the Poem

I have become the poem,
questions never completely answered.
Ambiguity in the clearest sense—
A rainfall of insights, wet
and wondering what's next,
and why.

Save me from myself, words!
Calm the storm in my veins.
It's never easy
wandering through the hours this curious.
At times, it's a fire walk.
Good thing I love fire.

If there's a wide-open space
in my mind,
I fill it with inquiry:

Why and where?
How much?
Until when?
Then what?
For whom?
Who cares?

I can't help but analyze the crap out of it.
I want all to reveal itself.

It's this obsession I have
with the minutiae.
Life is in the details,
where essence comes alive.

When I am inside the words,
I am free of all worry and earthly concerns.

—Gina Mazza

An Adventure Inward

Creativity is an ocean voyage,
a rocket launch into space:
Vast and somewhat unfathomable,
heights and depths immeasurable.

That's the fun of it—
An adventure inward.

This planet is a great big ball of excitement
and Dickenson never left her room—
yet saw more of the world than most.

Travel gives context; it is good for that.
But where I'm going,
there is no map
or known mode of transportation.

No two itineraries are the same:
Point A to Point B to Point C doesn't exist.
The way is made on faith,
but like I said,
that's where joy hides, coyly.

Today I lift off
into the wild blue yonder
of stillness.

Silence and poetry
are synonymous, in a way:
Both keep me from being deluded
by the outer noise

that threatens to make me believe
things about myself
that just aren't true.

—Gina Mazza

When the Muse Arrives

When the Muse arrives,
I want to grasp onto her desperately
like a lover leaving
on a transatlantic sojourn.

"Take me with you!" I plead.
"Don't leave me stranded on the pier."

But I didn't bring a suitcase.
I wasn't aware we were leaving.

Soul travel can be erratic that way.
All you can bring is a compass
and a dream of the
destination that is calling.

Better to not be dragged down by a carry-on
when the Muse comes a courting.

In these moments,
simple pen and paper
become more precious
than platinum and gold—
and everything I need.

—Gina Mazza

Poetry is My Pulpit

Poetry is my pulpit.
Congregate, and feel
genius rising from it.

Sense the surge between sentences.
If your heartbeat quickens,
your blood races faster,
prose has done its work:
The adrenaline of love—
fearless and free.

Emerson and Whitman would be pleased.
They have been trying to tell us all along:

"Rise up!
Recite a new creed.
Only you can do it.

Don't wait for instructions.
None are needed to flip the switch.
Just read these words and awaken!"

—Gina Mazza

Slow Rush

Poetry may not say what the answer is.
It has no desire to be that obvious.
But the answers are there,
inherent in the unwritten.

It's not an intellectual exercise.
Rather, a soul murmur through the body.
Just hum along.
If you don't know the lyrics,
tap your foot to its rhythm.

True word play is not about mastery,
but rather, fidelity—
coming to place of honesty
with yourself,
genuflecting when you feel the need
to pause and ponder.

It's a slow rush.
Take your time
and fly as high as you dare.
Linger over the prose,
as if studying your face
reflected in a cool pond
on a summer's day.

Ripple with curiosity.

Peer into the depths,
not looking for anything, necessarily.
Just observe the curvature
and subtle motion of thought waves
as they break on the surface.

Use your mind as the tool it is:
an instrument for adhering meaning,
a fine-toothed sawblade
slicing through murkiness
to reveal hidden roots in the mud,
solid ground beneath fluidity.

—Gina Mazza

Dare to Write the Unspeakable

Writers, I feel you.
We share an unspoken bond.
Words, to us, are freedom
pleasure,
truth,
astonishment,
remedy,
laughter,
angst,
revelation.

We tremble at every syllable
as it pours forth into
a chalice of delight.
We drink in every curve and detail.

Want to change the world?
Pick up your pen.

Dare to write the unspeakable.
Let what needs to be known
come to light.

—Gina Mazza

Home

What is Home

What is Home but a sacred altar
upon which to lay your head,
where all things make sense.

There's no true refuge from this world
but there is the pious assemblage of a place
that gives us rest.

There, we love those we love best
and through daily actions,
demonstrate the curative power of presence,
of simply being with another.

"I am here for you," Home says,
and you mirror this same vow
to your beloveds.

Home, in all your humility,
thank you for welcoming me.
I prostrate myself at your threshold.

Your walls speak of contentment;
floorboards echo the chorus.

Pantry, stacked with spices,
mason jars of tree nuts,
and midnight snacks for dreaming,

bless me with your promise of nourishment
for seasons to come.

Even Mudroom, where I launder my clothes,
endeavors to purify me of disquiet.

Nearly every day,
I ascend the steps
to my upper sanctuary,
a measured procession
towards the Muse,
who lures me
with her spectral refrain.

In this loft,
creativity is created,
peacefully,
in its own time,
as cows lumber
along the cattle path,

a stone's throw from Desk,
who holds all my secrets.

'Tis a good day to be Home.

—Gina Mazza

Simple Blessings

Birds in trees.
Laughter while snuggling
on the couch with my love.

Chili in the crock and
banana-nut bread wafting
from the oven.

Waylon on the Wi-Fi.
A phone call from a friend.

Dappled sunlight through
linen drapes,
a clean bathroom,
knowing where my slippers wait.

Daffodils sneak-peaking
along the wood's edge.
Neighbors honking
as they cruise by and holler
"How ya'll doin?"

It's glorious just to have a home
to come home to,
with beauty all around
and blessings too high to count.

—Gina Mazza

Code Blue

There's a seat at the table
for anyone who wishes
to discuss salvation.
These are conversations
not easily had.
Opinions stack like bricks
and threaten to crush
the spirit of the dialogue.

You were given intellects
for a reason.
Use them to whittle out
of the prison you've erected.

It's 11:58.

You can spend these precious seconds
arguing there's no clock.
Still, that doesn't stop
progress or regress.

It's a joke to assume that we can deny
the faculties of nature.
Wishful rationales can be catastrophic.
These times necessitate critical thinking.

Planet Earth is a sentient being

but it's not emotional that way.
It's not up for debate.
She is going to respond like
any living thing:
with an aim towards self-preservation,
whatever that requires.
Floods
tornadoes
rock slides
heat waves
avalanches
earthquakes
tsunamis

are not punishment for how we've abused our home;
It's simply nature's response to the degradation,
a means to restore balance.

Restorative—not punitive. Get that?

Think of it this way:
If someone coveted your major organs,
assuming you didn't need them,
what would you do?
Deny they were taken?
Litigate the thievery?
Politicize the violation?
Or get yourself to triage before you code blue?

Save humanity from its own carnage—
not just of the human species—
all species,

none of which are less than us.
We are only one part of this creation—
not the all,
and not all that.
We can stop the bleeding
or succumb to our own pathology.

We need nature.
Nature doesn't need us.

—Gina Mazza

Stand Down Tyranny

By now, actually, we've gone beyond logic.
Reasons have their place
but they have limits.

Haven't we long grown bored with being
mesmerized
catholigized
homogenized
catastophized
hyper-sensitized?

Step up to a higher version of worlds,
where love begins and never ends.
Time passes on its axis
as wild birds fly
across a patient sky,
aware of the grandeur of it all—
are we?

Stand down tyranny.
It has no place on this new earth.

Now we are all about
the ecstasy of breath,
the wonderment of moments
lived without fear

of personal retribution.

Will you join me?

—Gina Mazza

What is Mine to Do?

Calling inward to my soul,
the time has come to resurrect.

Sound the clarion bells above my head.
Help me reach beyond myself
to see the greater light.

Sometimes I ache
for the heart of this world.
It weighs on me
like a loomed skirt
lined with iron.

If there's something
I should be doing,
if something
is mine to do,
inspire my steps
towards it.

Open the window
of my mind
so I might see it.

Release the shackles that
bind me to sameness.

Arouse my boldness
to contribute the gifts
bestowed on me
before entry into this
paradise lost.

—Gina Mazza

Death

What Happens When We Die?

What happens when we die?
Are we slurped up
by the quantum cauldron,
recontextualized,
and spit back out
as another substance?

Does the Big Wooden Ladle
of creation swirl us
into other forms
with a sonorous
"Ta-Da!"?

Death:
another journey
into the unknown—
or is it?

Turns out,
life is good preparation—
at least how we're doing it.
We die a little
every day.

Maybe that's why
we break

each other's hearts:
to brace for
the inevitable.

—Gina Mazza

Let's Eat Ice Cream Bars

Let's eat ice cream bars
in the hot sun
without napkins.

When life runs and gets sticky,
we'll lick it off our hands
with pleasure.

The funeral march
will start soon enough.

For now,
we turn
toward the warmth
and devour
the cool sweetness
of these days.

—Gina Mazza

End Times

Could it be
the end times are upon us?
The end of

dispensability
debauchery
baseless suffering
nonaccountability
excuses for uncaring
Schadenfreude
cognitive dissonance
short-sightedness
cultism
hypocrisy
idolatry

decimating what doesn't belong to us
assuming anything without heart listening
messing with our blessing.

Let's hope and pray
it's the end times.

—Gina Mazza

POEMS BY SCOTT A. TERRELL

"When you shovel the crap out of your life, everything stops stinking."

—Scott A. Terrell

Ascension

The Ascension Song

"Stop ranting and watch,"
she softly said.
The wave calmed its
angry snarl.
The lion looked up from its meal.
The fierce paused.

The tiny child rose from her birth
and hummed a new tune.

Inside of the lyrics of
absolute innocence is
simply Absolute.

Across the whole world
a new song became alive
with peaceful vibrancy.

War became angered as even
his belligerence was touched.

The crack in the bell was healed
and Liberty rang out with a glad shout.
Worship arose from the mouths
of the mad throng.

Unyielding, the tiny voice rose clear

into the angel's chorus,
joining them in harmonious symphony.

"It has begun!" said the Divine.

The piercing light of love spread
throughout the whole Earth and beyond.
Nothing of darkness could stand firm as itself
and was consumed within the light of
this omnipotence.

A light shone from Earth Mother
like no other,
seen from beyond all time and space
as Karma itself was consumed
in the roaring kiln of a
new race having chosen Love.

One Voice, One Light, One Love,
One Heart sang its loveliness
upon the universe.

Seven billion voices opened
their hearts in a song
of mighty bliss, releasing
unto the universe the perfection
of its true purpose.

The angels wept as they witnessed
the ascension of humankind.
Time collapsed and became
one with the song.

The Reaper of Grim Death laid
down his scythe and opened
his hall of records. It vanished
inside of the bliss-filled note.

Everyone, Every when, Everywhere
joined the chorus of light.
War became calm,
surrendered his arms forever,
and joined the glad shout.

"Listen," she softly said.
Everyone, Every when, Everywhere
listened with incredulous joy
as the tiny tot on unsteady
legs hummed with
her true voice . . .
the Ascension Song.

—Scott A. Terrell

Surrender

Oh God,
my eyes rest upon Thy
wondrous beauty.
Ever my thoughts dwell
within Thy presence.

Let my heart stand inside your own:
loving with fervor,
caring with kind solace,
judging not the efforts of others,
accepting peace as the norm.

Let me see the beauty that inhabits
the greatness of humanity.
Help me cherish that beauty, as do you.

Inspire me to surrender to the
seed of faith planted in my bosom,
nourished by Thy fiery breath of life.

Marry me close to Thy cause.
Adopt me into Thy glory.
Let my heart feel only goodness.
Sight my eyes with Thy perfect beauty.

Roar into my ears Thy eternal word.
Create in me a zeal for growth.

Allow Thy Hope to overpower my fear.
Are you not greater by all stretches of imagination?

Gift me with Thy potent heart pierce
so that I can envision the heart of a self-traitor,
releasing him from that bondage.

Overcome my stubborn resistance
with Thy patient surrender.
Blend my will with yours in harmonious symphony
so I can endure all change,
all growth, all persevering
with gentle calm,
resting in steadfast acceptance
of the path set before me.

Empower my word with Thy word
so that all evil flees before me, unable
to stand against Thine in dwelling light.

I have accepted the brokenness set before me,
down to the barest husk of dry spirit.

Rebuild me with the heart of Christ
as my center stone.
I plead with you for all there is
for me to want to know,
knowing that Thy ears never sleep.

Above all, create these things
with the forgiveness and love of Christ.

Cause an unstoppable force of light
to resurrect the true worth of all mankind
from the ashes of defeat and despair.

Merge my thoughts into fluidity
instead of harsh, rigid focus.
Create me as a model that inspires
a deep, long burn in humanity to reach
for the beauty of true worth.

Mold my thoughts and words into an
impeccability that stands the test of time,
flowing from the river of life itself.

To your end, I give this beseeching.
To your glory, I commend my path.
To the betterment of humanity
I place myself into
Thy heart, Thy hands.

Open Thy path to forge me as Thy will.
Amen.

—Scott A. Terrell

The Great Empty

I have grown to know that You
are in the looking,
but cannot be seen.

I know that You
are not out there
in the stars—
although they are in You.
You cannot be found
within my essence—
Although my essence
is completed in You.

I am lost within
this new understanding—
abandoned and worse than dead,
for I know that
death is irrelevant.

Where are you Now?
What is left for me to cherish?

My strong anchor
has broken its chain
with illuminated truth—
a false anchor that believed

You needed something
from me for Your joy.
A shift indeed.
From lost to found, from
ego to illumination.

The great empty has been opened
to Your lead. So, speak!
I stand waiting for my fate.

"My Son, my wonderful, precious son,
you understand so much,
you grasp so little.
Do you not know I am You?
I am found behind the
door of surrender.
Shake off those shackles that bind the Glory
to the feeble spark of doing.

My son, be the vastness
of the miracle that is life itself.
Immerse yourself in that miracle.
Just hold fast to the simple
Joy that is inherent in life.
Release yourself into the natural state
of the whirling dervish.
Within chaos is calm.
At the center of the spin
stands the still point
that cannot be moved
by any means.

The Great I Am
is ready to shed her cloak,
and in that shedding
Love is discovered
as the binding force that is in
all things, holds all things,
feeds all things, heals all things,
hopes and is forever
inherently changeless.
Come to Me—
for in becoming
love, you are
becoming God.

The Great Door stands at
the ready for the final shattering.
Let the batter of the rams begin.
Are you truly seeking Truth?
It shall always find her seeker
and in that finding,
Eternity is waiting."

—Scott A. Terrell

Gratitude

I have heard my voice
speak truth to others.
Yet that voice was
really speaking to me.
It reduces me to rubble,
a wisp of smoke,
a tear-filled ghost,
a vacuum wanting to
escape its own void.

Inside of that quiet I stand firm,
knowing that the inside whisper will
speak its holy truth.
"In all things be grateful," the whisper said.
"Even in sorrow love exists in its purest state."

The whisper continued:

"A solid foundation can be built
only where impurities have been washed away
by the salt of a tear.
Inside of that place of sacred surrender,
the angels wait to do their work of filling
your empty heart.
That filling shall consist of substance.
Nothing outside of spirit can shake your faith
when it is grounded so.

You shall walk with a knowing
that holy purpose lights your way.
All seeking shall come to an end,
for you have found the truth that tells you
that all you need, all you seek,
already stands firm within."

—Scott A. Terrell

Freedom

A Simple Choice

I look out across the valley of shadow,
knowing that my commitment to fear
has brought me to this place of sorrow.

Having that knowing in my bosom
frees me to act.
On hallowed ground do I plow
a furrow for planting.

I know in my wretched heart
that a greater power
has given me the key to freedom,
a simple choice:

Reject my commitment to fear,
or keep it.
Affirm my commitment to love,
or not.

A hollowed furrow rips its path
across my shattered heart,
preparing it for a pure seed,
plucked from the tree of life itself.

Fear—a dark, wrenched master,
or a kind, protective friend;
a simple choice

that will change everything.
Found in a tiny pup that
quakes its body in greeting;
he is the savior of the world, modeled to me;
my God loving me through this tiny pup.
His kind of love cares for naught
except a gentle hand,
a shattered heart.

How could I choose to fear
a God of love?
Yet, I chose a life of sorrow
for a God of fear,
who peers from my blinded eyes.

At last, I have been given sight
into the root of pain
that is the source of my misery.
A simple choice that can change my world.

Sprouting a harvest unto no other,
born from a shallow grave,
where I buried my God of fear,
where he waits to rear his life
once again in my fertile heart.

Love is my power to conquer
the enemy of hope.
Gratitude floods my essence
with the dawning of that hope,
lit with the flame of newfound peace.

—Scott A. Terrell

Salt of the Sea

Have you ever cried with sheer gratitude
for all you have?
For all that has been seemingly withheld?

Have you cried in gratitude
for a friend who thinks of you,
prays for you, holds you in their faith
when you have none of your own?

Have you cried for the possessions
that support your way of life, ones
that most in the world know nothing about?

Have you ever cried with complete acceptance
of everything just the way it is?

Have you ever cried because the
vast lonely that you feel
is far better than a heartbreak
grounded in accepting less than you deserve?

Have you cried with gratitude for your family
that somehow accepts you
in unconditional understanding
that you are perfect just as you are?

Have you cried in absolute peace despite the conditions
of a seemingly intolerable condition of your life?

Have you cried in joy knowing that
in spite of your ego, all is well?

I am crying tonight.
I will cry tomorrow.
I will cry for you.
Love is all there is.

My tears blend with the salt of the sea.
They are in good company.
Somewhere in that ocean,
the tears of the Beloved join with my own.

—Scott A. Terrell

True Love

Pledging Kindness

I pledge with my utter being, with eternal fire,
to allow kindness to flower from my inner sanctum.
May it bring forth sweet nectar
for all who dare to taste its glory.

Within that kindness is the true love
I have sought for all of my life.
Does not kindness bring forth its due?
A kind heart cannot bring forth a scowling face.

My life is worth less than dust without this depth.
I will have wasted all breath as if less than a worm.
I gladly grasp this gift and fly to the distant stars,
for even they know about kindness.

In that flying, I shall know God's true heart,
the essence of true love.
Inside true love is the Great I Am
that acts only in perfect kindness.
The closer I fly, the less separation I perceive,
and the more real I truly become.

I place my foot squarely on the holy path
that solidifies this dream.
Hate cannot exist in this holy glory.
My surrender is complete.

Today, eternity gains it's just due.
I start my peace-filled rest,
planted in God's perfect kindness.
Let me bear fruit in absolute glory.
In this heaven, I surrender to
essential peace at long last.

—Scott A. Terrell

A Tiny Flea

I cannot know the wisdom of the pen
or the love of God.
Both are beyond mind.

I cannot understand the depth of that love.
Can you understand gravity,
or light, or warmth?

Where has this seeking taken
me except into greater mysteries,
and a deeper understanding of
my small whimperings?

Yet in some unfathomable way,
inside of my small self,
is the entirety of God.
Somehow, he cares about my suffering.

I cannot understand how a vast being
of absolute perfection can even notice
a tiny flea—
yet I do not need to understand
to accept that truth.

Acceptance opens God's heart
to a storehouse of mighty riches!
A treasure of peace!

A golden locket of love.
Engraved angels needing to serve.

"Who am I?" I ask the Inside Whisper.
"God's reason for being," is the answer.
"That makes no sense to me!"
I weep.

"Love doesn't need sense; only acceptance,"
the Whisper continues.

"When you thank God for a moment in time,
does He not want to give you more of those moments?

When your heart leaps at the soft touch of your beloved,
does not God's heart leap as well?

When your life is his life,
when your heart is his heart and
when your will is in alignment with God,
are you not, in a very real sense,
an expression of His perfection?

Is God good to himself?
Does he create more of his own beauty?

Does God love himself?
Is God's beauty reflected everywhere?

You are more than you know.
Your path has taken you into the heart of the Beloved!

How can that absolute reflection of love
not inhabit all that you are,
all that you express, all that you feel?

Is not that reflection mirrored
back to the source of that reflection?
When God sees you, He sees himself.

This is the truth of the heavens.
When so many do not see or notice that love,
that part of God is silent, in grief.

This grief is reflected back
to the source of that grief—
a tiny flea."

—Scott A. Terrell

Begging Cup

I am God's empty begging cup.
He is filling me with riches unseen,
pouring out heaven's floodgates.

I am a threadbare coat on a rotten stick.
My chest window is open,
waiting for words from God's heart.

The warmth of knowing God's love
burns all of my emptiness into joy.

Who needs more wine?
These heart musings make my head spin!
At least with wine,
there is a reason that makes sense!

—Scott A. Terrell

I Know Love

As a child, I told myself,
"No one loves me,"
and, sadly, it was true.

Today I know better yet
the question remains:
"What is love?"

I know love in the eyes
and soul of Bailey Dog.
His eager, patient,
pure love pours from
his gentle soul.
Unquestioning, perfect,
unwavering, eternal.

I know love in the eyes
of my grandchildren when they run
screaming into my arms,
looks of delight upon their faces.

I know the love of a friend
who is always there for me,
answering my phone calls,
listening to my broken heart,
pouring forth fresh anguish at
the latest betrayal.

I know the love of a daughter
who still calls me Daddy
and thrills my soul with
heart wonder.

I know the love of my sponsor
who has guided me into
the beauty I am today,
always there for me, always
faithful, unwavering, loyal.

I know that the power of the twelve steps
is a true love that can bring
me back from the dark storm of despair.

I know that it is *not* love to accept your lover
back from the arms of another
with an excited wag of the tail and happy barks—
It is addiction.

And now I know another kind of love.
I accept this lesson at long last.
I shall call it: I love me.

—Scott A. Terrell

Fire

Not Today

I am going to die someday;
but not today.
How?
Why?
When?

Someday.
What does that mean?
It means that my mission
is not finished.
The Word has not completed
its speaking as me.

When, then?
Not for me to know.
I shall just rise as a phoenix
and begin to speak as Eternity's proxy,
as I always have.

There is a truth that all seek
to know, to become,
to advance inside the Kingdom.
And when that fire burns to ash,
all of the lies of the shadow,
then rest shall come
and peace will inhabit
the soul of humankind at long last.

"What fire?" I ask.
"The Holy Fire of Jerusalem inhabited
by Moses and King David," is the reply.

"Yet there is more," speaks the Holy Pen.
"There is one consecrated to raise into life
all that are dead to the Holy Word."

What?
What?
What?
Today? Now?

"When you see, knowing shall blossom into holy fire."

"But I may perish with a disease," I lament.

"Nonsense," is the roared reply.
"Do the work required of all saints and
everything shall be added to your account."

"Wake up and rise above your perceived sorrow!
You shall finally come into the majesty
that has been reserved for you and you alone."

So, I wept,
and wept,
and wept again,
and rose from my bed of perceived misery.
Tears of shame fled my heart and soul.

I picked up the Poet Society's Pen

and began to write the holy word.
This very day, the phoenix rose
and illuminated the holy pen
that eased the shadow's mark upon
the heart of humankind,
leading the way to peace.

—Scott A. Terrell

Fire of Creation

I live in the fire of creation,
always immersed in
studied thought,
bringing to life objects
to serve the whims
of humankind:

Objects of beauty
made of wood, metal,
tempered steel.

The fire of creation
molds me into a mirror of itself—
the purity of love, beauty,
tempered flesh;
a dragon that brings
to life the fire of Word.

The fire of creation brings
forth the building of souls.
The beauty of humankind
is a reflection of the purest love.

So have I become love at long last?
God is love; does that mean
that I have melded into whom
I was created to be?

We shall see.

In the beginning was the
fire of Creation, Purest Love.
One, the same.
I like this path that leads to the
heart of Creation,
filled with angel feathers,
rose petals, inspiration.

Grateful, I am.
Grateful, I shall stay,
filled with the power of Divine Word.
I tread softly upon the holy
path of miracles, knowing that
the fire of Creation lights the way.

I did not ask for, nor did I earn,
this honor of service.
The fire of Creation chose me.
I simply said yes.

—Scott A. Terrell

Integrity Candle

Arrogance is a cruel friend.
It thinks that no one can see
a lying heart, a false smile,
a guilt-drenched soul.

Justifying is a poor companion.
It looks outside of itself,
never within.
It cannot see that its foundation is
based on an illusion.

Projecting issues upon another
and not facing my immaturities
has left me alone, immersed
within my own sorrow,
like a single candle in a dark cave.

If integrity is the cave,
and the candle is my sorrow,
the light must be my salvation—
and my loss, the reason
for illumination.

Yet a fierce fire can start from a
single flicker of that candle.

Burn this dross from my heart.

Let the purity of golden wonder
shine into my healing.

My intention to become
all that I was created to be
begins here, now,
with this integrity candle.

One flicker, one thought,
one choice at a time.

—Scott A. Terrell

Healing

Inventory

Can you go down through your brokenness
into that vast empty hole of who you are not
and reach farther still into your soul?

Can you ask for healing,
knowing your powerlessness?

Can you pick yourself up, dust yourself off,
and journey with your soul for once?
Or will you stay in your self-pity
and take everyone around you down too?

Can you confront an abuser in love and compassion,
giving only hope and direction, if asked?

Can you see a monster in the mirror,
release your fear and choose to heal that monster?
Can you love that horror
during the broken agony of failure?

Can you choose brokenness over ego,
letting go of your need for self-importance,
or will you half-live your life
looking outside instead of within?

Do you know that for every question you've ever asked,
the answer lies within,
or do you accept others' truths as your own?

Can you let go of the falseness of passion
that masquerades as love, and be true to yourself?

Do you hope for your dreams in faith,
or do you hoard them like a miser,
until they shrivel and die?

Can you wait on love until you become
someone that you love,
knowing that love will come in its own time?
Are you willing to do what it takes, as long as it takes,
to be someone you want to be with?

Can you embrace the gift of pain,
reject the power of blame,
and see the spirit of healthy shame?

Can you see that the shameless behavior of others
is not about you,
and yours is not about them?

Can you look into your soul with amends in your heart?
Can you look at your past with the same?

Can you forgive yourself and use the experience
to teach others the way?

Are you willing to die today,
cry for the past,
laugh in your hope,
live in the moment,
or love with wild abandon—
regardless of the risk?

—Scott A. Terrell

Potent Truth

I have looked far and wide,
searching the globe for thy perfect heal.

I have withdrawn in deep silence
and studied long in that frantic inquiry.

I have entrusted others in caring
for my heart, an impossible chore.

I have not considered that your gift
was already there, inherent in my being.

It has been waiting in patient calm
for the unveiling of vast completion.

In that long search, I have missed
the truth of my divine essence and all it entails.

Driving that search was the chronic pain
of illusion, of perceived separation.

"Love is pain."
"Love is betrayal."
"Love is abandonment."
What torrid lies I have convinced of myself.

In truth, all I have, all I need

already exists within simply being.
My heart always has been, always will be,
tightly held, eternally blessed,
divinely inspired.

Love, sweet-potent heal,
you are not in the looking.
You cannot be found or even sought after.
Inside that search, the frantic toss of
unsettled waves disrupt the harmonious
orchestration of simply being.

I accept you, oh potent truth.
I will simply be and exist in the
ecstatic moment of eternal bliss.

Inherent in simply being,
life itself is evoked in a celebration
of perfect love.

—Scott A. Terrell

God Forgives

Beside the tree at Calvary,
people came to pray.
Inside the tree at Calvary,
angels came to weep.

They could not know—
how could they know—
the lesson they brought
to the Messiah, or
the one he brought to them.

Forgiveness . . . Forgiveness
was the last sacred intention
bled from his soul.
At the end, the very end, he
forgave all that man had done.

His tears, his blood, his love
melted his Father's heart.
God's wrath was turned aside
and he forgave the truly unforgivable.

Christ did not come to save the world.
He came to set his Father free.
Inside of that purity, even the heart
of God was cleansed.
Inside of that cleansing

rests the salvation of mankind.
Inside the tree at Calvary—
eternally rooted in love—
stands firm the lesson,
the power of love,
and the gift of Christ.

—Scott A. Terrell

POEMS BY DONNA KNUTSON

"Beauty does not require perfection; in fact, it lives and breathes so beautifully in the wilds of imperfection."

—Liezel Graham

Prayer

Feeling Safe

Oh, Most Holy God,
at the end of the day
it is good to feel safe, warm, content.

To be able to recall the joys of the day.
The tiny moments that warmed the heart.
The hope that still beats within
and the people who helped bear witness to love.

At the end of the day,
it is good to hear important news.
The language of love spoken in words.

The lightness of heart when the doctor gives answers
or the struggle doesn't seem so lonely.
Someone shows up,
gives a hug,
looks you in the eye, and
reassures that things will be alright.

It is good to be present, to pray,
to provide a chair when one needs to sit down.
To be held up by strong arms,
wise words, a listening ear.

It is good to let go of the chores remaining
after a long day. To quit and lie down.

To find comfort in Rocky Road ice cream and
an old movie.
To scroll through famous quotes, photos
of another time.
To remember where we have come from, and how far,
like a star falling from the sky
and the gigantic moon sitting up so high.

At the end of the day,
it is good to be free of complaints
and to listen with compassion.
To throw a blanket up to one's chin and
close one's eyes on the hours.

It is good to leave worry and to remember
the expansiveness of the spirit of the Living God
and to give gratitude for this one day,
this one gift that only you could see
from inside the heart of God.
Amen and amen.

—Donna Knutson

Solo Piece of Light

Every morning,
before mind finds an edge of veil
to open in the daylight,

there is a smooth shadow and silent sound,
a night time of street lamps,
a ritual of God on the roof.

Before stars go to sleep
and sun kisses the moonlight goodnight,

enter in . . .
sideways if you must.

No one you know will be there,
in between the Here and Now.

Thread of knowing,
breath of God.

Kneel close enough to hear the sigh,
this solo piece of Light.

—Donna Knutson

Known

Sometimes people will tell me
there is no God.
I can understand how they might feel that way,
but God in not a feeling, a nicety or a
napping through life's glory.

God is known, or else God is not
experienced in a second of living transcendent light,
or talking to a holy tree,
a blossom fallen on the kitchen counter,
bathing a baby,
standing silently near a grave
remembering the love that kept you alive
when there was simply
a spoonful of soup for the soul.

There are plenty of hours to touch the stars,
to anoint a child,
to bless the mailman,
to wave wonders with your wand,
plenty of ways to bow inside your Kingdom of Light.

You can try all of your life to keep God in a bottle
or thrown out to the sea,
packaged in tight thoughts or disturbed in your dreams;
but Rumi had some good thoughts
and Carl Jung knew a few things.

There are days of transcendence and days of darkness;
but how holy is that!
God appears everywhere and in everything.

—Donna Knutson

I Want

There is nothing wrong with saying
I want there to be millions of stars
in the sky when I die,
for my grandchildren to know
the words Magnificent and Majesty.

For the Divine Feminine to balance the energies
that will break through selfishness
to melt like honey into forgotten Wisdom.

I want there to be labyrinths in the woods
and behind churches.
For nature to nurture what heals broken vessels
and beads of rain to wash down into the core land,
into the clay, down into the soul land
where I preach way too much about beauty
and Oneness.
I want there to be shorelines that are rocky still.
For mountaintops to hold ledges for goats
and forgotten galaxies that can only be seen in the dark.

For chaos to be more about illumination
and right action
than wars and religion felt by the solitary soul,
imagined by saints and sinners
before they bow down to the ground

and the texture of dirt and remembrance to be filled
with purple crocus bulbs
on the other side of winter's storm.

I want for this simple, non-ordinary time
to be filled with revelation.

—Donna Knutson

Prayers on the Move

Oh, Most Holy God,
how many prayers have been said
on our way to somewhere?

When we are pregnant with life,
when lost in the world,
when content with a simple meal?

How many prayers have been said
on our way to speak hope,
to listen through tears,
to respect one another?

How many prayers have been said
on our way to deliver news,
to exclaim new life,
to releasing the past?

How many prayers have been said
on our way to praise a new day,
to load the car trunk with diapers,
to drop off medicine to a poor family,
to bake one more loaf of bread?

How many prayers have been said
in this season of men, women and children
who gather to witness with tinsel and silver bows,

to celebrate with food on the table,
and discussions that halt war and
what of Christ's love is birthing in the world?

May we whisper silently with
gratitude in our Mary of hearts
for the resilience to walk on this way.

—Donna Knutson

Simplicity

These days, I look for simplicity,
like the rain or words of grace and mercy
in poetry and scriptures,
the sounds of children.

I like noting the challenges,
being part of a wider picture,
praying for countries I will never see,
whispering blessings to strangers on the street,

counting Christ as Savior and
Buddha as relief of suffering;
numbered Beatitudes and Commandments
I memorized as a child and, as a teenager,
the wisdom of Kahil Gibran and e.e. cummings.
"I carry your heart with me, I am never without it ..."
could only be speaking of God.

And surely when we spoke the 23rd Psalm
at a child's funeral—
"He leadeth me beside the still waters.
He restoreth my soul ..."
held me in sacred space of healing light.

These days, I look for simplicity,
like the dog asleep on my bed,

the relationships I immerse myself in,
baptizing moments, the way
I answer happily to the name, "Hey, Mama."

This season of in-between and moving through
is just another cycle in a day where there is no time
and the miracles are just what I dreamed of as a child,

that gifts are given,
wooden boxes hold memories,
and every day I can light a candle
and give gratitude for the life that has been given.

—Donna Knutson

Down in the Belly

God goes down in the belly,
the gut of my longing for holy moments,
whale moments, wandering solo
and transformed moments.

Not caffeine-ingested moments, but those
trembling and terrifying "God has seen it all" moments
that redeem the surrendering, slim silhouette
of a woman's body,
that form of flesh I know, living close to the bone.

When sparrows speak and I listen.
Where voice has volume and velocity
and yet I whisper low to the ground,
where the grandmothers die
and the drums keep a beat.

I hear, you hear
the way we must go
to the depths of the belly,
where the God of fire and the God of peace
lives in the empty hollow of the cave in my dreams.

And if I am to worship from the heart of a woman,
let the curve of my hips and flash of my heart
ignite the warrior of my wounds and
the wisdom of God's way.

Let the borders come down and the brilliance remain!
May the charlatans renounce their claim
on any false gods
that desire room in the temple of my being.
May the swoon of my heart
shower light throughout the universe
and all that carries light from the darkness
to the heavens
touch the world with torches of flame
and fierce passions of God lust.

Holy healing that births compassion
way down in the belly of my soul.

—Donna Knutson

It's Good to be Holy

It's good to be Holy,
to walk a hundred miles without giving or taking,
to stand in the woods at the center of a grove of
white pines and say nothing at all,
to find space where community is taller than you are
and boughs that rise to heights you will never reach—
or maybe you will.

It is good to be Holy,
to walk a hundred miles dropping anxiety and
needing forgiveness,
just melting into emptiness by lowering one's head.

Weaving right, then left as the damp earth,
pelted with rain,
then frozen with ice, draws one deeper into the forest.

It is good to be Holy,
to walk a hundred miles reciting Rumi,
memorized from years of fiery flames and
Meister Eckhart's vision that finally became Home.

It is good to be Holy,
to know that inquiry sets our feet on a worthy path,
that Light is more than a lamp but the life
lived of the Holy.

—Donna Knutson

Dangerous Prayers

I said one of my dangerous prayers.
You know, the ones that change your life,
the ones you can't live without.

Whispering through the heart just before the dawn,
cardinals beginning their chatter in the
weeping mulberry
outside my bedroom window, catching sight of
a red wing before the blind is fully opened.

Prayers, once uttered, are gone … and
that exciting trembling
greets me in the middle of my gut.
How will the desires of my heart appear this time?

The way Spirit meets matter, trees leaning towards light,
children growing up and away,
we are given second and third chances at life.

No one seems surprised anymore that spells
can be broken and people are healed,
that we are battling for freedom,
that snowdrops bloom the day we have leap year.

We have grown steady in what we see
as pushing through obstacles,
finding the rose amidst the thorns,

moving our feet into Mystery.

Praying dangerous prayers that are answered
in perfect timing,
experiencing Light as a normal, daily occurrence.
Hard not to believe the veil is thinning.
The stories are Pentecostal,
like a radical, fiery consuming,
hearing Spirit on our own tongues.

There's something soothing about power that knows
its own body through awakening,
that hears from beyond while present,
that contains the Source while walking the ordinary
and praying dangerous prayers.

—Donna Knutson

If I Stop Praying

If I stop praying,
I'll lie down and rest too long.
I'll want to sleep instead of
rising to the colors of a new day.

I'll stop listening.
I'll forget how to bow in humility.

If I stop praying,
I'll think it's just me in the world,
alone and in madness,
instead of in the community of others.

So, I pray day in and day out,
Spirit holding ground beneath my feet,
pressing on the muscles of my heart,
circling round and round where peace has bent so low
there is no division between my life and yours.

I pray because I'm not afraid
to stand,
to shelter,
to walk beside,
to lean against,
to die for another.

I pray because I believe

it is possible
to open my arms,
to break with my heart,
to sing while I cry,
to lead while I stand.

I pray because there is wisdom
to simply be heard and honored.

—Donna Knutson

Prayer Walkers

Prayer walkers are as common as angels these days,
holding up signs for freedom,
resting near the trunks of redwood trees,
molding citizens of clay,
humming melodies with three and four parts,

asking the radically difficult questions of our time
while sinking into the arms of community.

Common with communion.
Pieces of bread scattered on the path.
Come this way.
Follow me.

There is a road to justice that will never
bypass the injured, the crying.
Thousands have walked it before;
we say it leads to the Holy, to freedom.

Many have marched it before
or walked it silently, reverently,
with an inner strength only a few master.

Wrap your arms around a tree, a friend.
Perform miracles while you can.
Be vulnerable with your heart, thoughts, needs.

Make up better stories than you've been told.
Be authentic like the tortoise, the whale, the sea.
Find refuge in friendships and strength in solitude.

Prayer walkers disguise themselves to no one.
Their path is clear.

An aura of Light permeates the Here and Now.
And all the Saints before walked it, too.

—Donna Knutson

Patience

No Arguing with Suffering

It has taken a long while to learn not to
argue with suffering.
To begin the day calmly.
To whisper a prayer.
To be grateful for light and the wing of a bird.
To plant trees next to river banks for children to climb.

To plant something yellow, then purple,
perhaps that pot of orange blossoms,
a white petal or two.

To write everything down with perfect black ink
on the back of an envelope or yellow writing pad,
then tossed into a drawer with the collection of mail.

It has taken a long while to learn
not to argue with suffering
but to capture the smiles, the mood,
the sacred memories.
To watch games children play and to smile
and not look back.

For we've been there, you and I,
on that cold winter hill
with snow and a shattering,
with roses and frozen tears,
with love left to give for another thirty years.

For every December we've had, then lost,
for every name I can list with a candle I have lit,
we will carry the memory
and the life once lived,
and hold love at the center
where the flame burns.

—Donna Knutson

Be Patient with God

Be patient with God,
with your expectations of healing and
your need to hurry the process.
Slow it down and the pieces appear.

Step into what is hard
what is horrible
what is shattering
about death and birth,
and baby animals born just before the second day
in the month of your longing.

Be patient with accidents of aging—
or were they awakenings, looking back?

It's okay to take a break and burn up in the pain.
To breathe less panic and more ease
of free air in the chest and lungs.

Transformation is one of those guilty pleasures,
a mystical wonder of the world,
something fairly close to daily miracles
and witnessing God on the sly.

It takes a long time to wear Beauty
but after a while, you are never without it.
Gray slacks and a pink cardigan sweater,

fluffy slippers and long white flowing hair.
The parts that seem so very hard
are really gifts of the ordinary.
And waking up seems rather slow,
like yellow paint on the walls or
a bell hanging in the library from a friend.

How do mystics make it this far?
And all around you, God stands
wondering alongside of you.

Reading the pages,
expanding the plot lines.
Widening the turns and corners
to which you'll walk.
While all the time,
God holding your hand.

—Donna Knutson

Love Changes

Do not be afraid
though love changes.

We are not meant to be the same
in the morning,
after prayer,
before confession,
after midnight when the ancients pass by,
during conversations with friends holding hot
chocolate.

Nor even after something old has died
and no one can find a baby to hold or
a prayer shawl to throw over your shoulders.

Do not be afraid
though love changes
who we are,
what we say,
how we serve.

Can we kneel to plant bulbs?
Will you wait at the hospital one more day?
Can you be love while love moves through
the healing in your hands?

Do not be afraid
when love is all you hear
and it is tiny, like blueberries in oatmeal,
and it is kind, like soft hugs from friends.

Do not be afraid
for lovers come in many forms
and some are there to surprise us,
and some are there to guide us.

But most are there to open us
to births we have not seen.

—Donna Knutson

Woven Shawls

What would it be like to see wisdom
worn as cloaks and rich woven shawls?
Threads of gratitude sewn into every glance
with the bold spine of surrender
pushing out the breath.

I have never known such a thirst as God brings on,
revealing the inner world of grace and beauty,
peace and justice.

That puppeteer pulling strings to push out the courage,
reminding us of the fierce love into which we are born.
The breathwork of desire hidden for such a short time
before revelation descends,
drawing the Light through skin and bone.

Thirsting for revelation,
pawing back what is not real,
burning through layers that built a wall,
seeking for worthiness when wonder will do.

How this Light sees through, sees through.

—Donna Knutson

Go Slow

Go slow in the summer.
Water the annuals in the dark.
Find the line in the sky with the stars and count them.

Point your finger to the clouds.
Raise your glass to the moon.
Say a prayer while sweeping the patio.
Bless the mail carrier as she delivers letters
across the states.

Go slow in the summer.
Pick just the right watermelon
and a cherry soda with bubbles,
a jar of spear pickles and a bag of peaches
from a truck bed in the parking lot.

Go slow in the summer.
When you walk the puppy in the park,
put the grandchildren onto swings,
push the bicycle up the hill and
flag down the ice-cream truck as it
comes around the corner.

Go slow in the summer.
Watch the rose unfold.
Write with pen and ink from a bottle.
Find a stamp with a heart that you love.

—Donna Knutson

Grief

Remembering After Grief

One day after a very long time of grief,
I woke up and remembered—

How water felt when I washed my hair,
fingers kneading the scalp,
baptized and born.

How lemons smelled and my tongue recoiled,
and I could see the red of a strawberry
and slice tiny pieces of banana and cantaloupe
for a tray in the garden.

One day after a very long time of grief,
I woke up and remembered—

Light crushing all resistance,
even the palms of my hands
healing and holy,
and the mind of the heart,
swirling in a consciousness that pulled back
a thousand veils all at once.

I woke up and rode on the revelation
for a very long time,
on the verbs and the sway of the Yes.

The insistence of following further
some radical desire of collecting jars
to hold the Light,
to set them near the sea
for others to follow.

—Donna Knutson

Do the Work

Maybe it took five years off my life,
I'll never truly know.
I just did the work and came out on the other side
content, healthier, free.

Maybe soul work is an avenue
or a degree to which one will work through
to find authenticity, less anger,
and truly live an uncompromising life.

Letting others off the hook,
fishing less for acknowledgment,
and enjoying the bright, white snow
resting on the tree limbs.

Maybe the hard work of actualization,
a myriad of moons and a Third Eye,
offers a threshold of opportunity,
a lens into failure and grief stains,
pillows crumpled up in the night.

A solo journey of God on the loose
will add a decade onto the life
of an earth child,
a sunset watcher,
a cave dweller,
a praise singer,

a healer who holds Grace
in the palm of her hand.

—Donna Knutson

Heaven

When I get to heaven or wherever
holy gods listen to our explanations
through tunnels of lights,
screens and projectors,
harps and harmonicas,
ukuleles and trombones,

I will not recite the poets I've loved
or the scripture I've read,
nor interpret the scribbles of my
children's first finger paintings.

I will not turn away from the questions I have
or the people who greet me:
my mom and my dad,
my daughter, Kate,
my dog, Rose, and the rest of the four paws;
my friends:
Elizabeth, who knew how to sing,
Ruth, who knew how to die well,
Kristen, who found me my first healer,
Fern, who taught me about grace,
Cedar, from seminary, who said God has wings
then left to find out,
Carolyn, with whom I swapped muses
under our desks.

I will not run and hide
as earthlings tend to do,
but I am sure I will cry—
for beauty of this world and the next tends to do that—
and falling down, no matter which realm
you've come upon,
tends to make one weak in the knees
and full in the heart;
there's a breaking in and opening out,
all at the same time.

And what was captured in
years of gratitude,
years of praise,
years of adoration,
will run down my face
as a life of deep struggle and joy.

—Donna Knutson

Compassion

Heal the World

If you lived as if you were here to heal this world,
long loved before you were born,
how would you use the volume of your voice?

How would you use the pain in your mind
to listen deeply and see the light in another's eye
instead of throwing your illusions onto them?

How would you worship this one day
while hanging twinkle lights in the trees
and staying true to your Higher Self?

Would you speak kindly,
enter homes with grace and peace,
leave your own agenda to be
one of deep consciousness?

So, continue your labors of beauty and hope.
Do your meditations that bring insightful wisdom.
Tell your stories while understanding
your life is only once given.

And review the daily wonders,
the revelations that set you apart
from those who are blind.

Stay close to the Light

while entering the room with your fire.

Remain pure where you have been
called to speak Truth.
Stay silent with those who have none.

Stand strong with the inner glow that
does not allow others to crush or condemn it.

Hold others' thoughts and words lightly
as they travel their own lives.

Open doors for your own beauty
while praying for healing and the
lightening of entwined souls.

—Donna Knutson

Breakdown

Some people think it's unusual
to have a breakdown.
How do you think one wakes up?

How do you think you heal
the traumas,
the losses,
the little deaths along the way
without letting go on the
deepest level possible?

This crack in the psyche
Jung describes as mystics walking edges
that only brave souls dare to go.

In the depths of the darkness
you find the steps,
the swirl of the staircase,
the use of energy to pull oneself up.

There you find the heart of God,
the help of a healer,
the nutrition needed to create a
healthy body and clear mind.

Shame disappears.

That injury gets pardoned.
This mercy is for everyone.

God becomes personal and known,
the breath and bone.
You are never alone.
Thoughts drift by as Spirit is
embodied, enlivened,
surviving all you've ever done.

When the morning sun touches a new day,
eternity continues and you begin again.

—Donna Knutson

Angel Pens

All the words that begin a story
sound like holy angels with pens lit on fire.

When meditation is done and the candles blow away
with a tiny puff and breath from the heart,
then I walk into the world,
down the neighborhood avenues,
through the church doors,
into the forests and fields.

With the rush of the streams
and dirt from the streets
and men with cardboard signs on the corner.

I hear the songs of a season,
feel the warmth of God's hand,
know the push of the Spirit,
carry the hope of a greater way.

I give the man a dollar bill,
open the door for a stranger,
toss out the old illusions and
live bolder in this land.

All the words that begin a story
sound like holy angels with pens lit on fire.

—Donna Knutson

Trust Your Ability to be Faithful

Trust your ability to be faithful.
You can still dream of saving the world.

I have prayer flags flying next to baby sleepers
and drawers of tiny white candles that
come out when the moon is full.

Trust your ability to find the heart of the world
within your own heart.

Hold onto the fact that God disturbs
and comforts almost simultaneously,
if not in complete synchronicity.

Trust your ability to be faithful,
no matter what the dream entails
or how far you have to go to see the Light.

There are those who point and
those who stand right at the edge.
Know you are about to enter the
realm of magnificence.

The tiniest movement is enough;
the shortest prayer,
the longest sigh,
the forbidden sentence,

the loudest cry.

Trust your ability to be faithful.
You are known
and your dream is the one
stirring up the world.

—Donna Knutson

Speak Your Truth

Speak your truth.
Walk into the sunset while on fire.

Claim the calamity of our times
while in conversation with woods and altars
covered with candles, peace pipes,
stoles of Muslims, Christians and Jews.

Prayer beads and sage burnt
to the north and the south,
east and the west;
healing swells of salvia stems.

Speak your truth,
entangled in a weary world
while standing tall,
not calling it right or wrong.

Find the friendships that you
won't break up with,
the beauty you cannot resist,
the transformation that you
will surrender to,
the call you will bow to.

The moment you dissolve into
the song of the cardinal,
you will be set free.

—Donna Knutson

Beauty

Sanctuary

May the coming year bring greater quiet
and confidence to your life.

May there be less striving and more sanctuary,
fewer holy heroes and one voice you recognize
as your own guiding Light.

May you capture the moments that melt your heart,
the boldness that becomes you,
the radiance that shines through your smiling eyes
and describes you as belonging to the Holy.

May the woods shelter your wisdom and the
sway of the trees bring peace to your resistance.

May you know you are adored
and made in an image that raises you up.

May you have faith to face the Mystery,
the challenges and the chaos on the
authentic path that speaks your name.

May you carry your friends and family lightly
so they, too, may grow.

May you create and follow the one true love

that sets your heart ablaze with the fire
of a life everlasting.

And in all of a day,
may you grow stronger and steadier,
lighter with laughter,
sound within the peace
that passes all understanding.

—Donna Knutson

Beauty

One day I woke up and she was buried contently.
Deep, deep in the wrinkles of my skin
and pondering of my mind.

She who had witnessed such loss, vision, harmony,
Transformation and clouds that opened like portals
to the world beyond and within.

One day she stopped bickering with beetles
to stay out of her house and carried seeds
to the setting sun and blew them into the mist.

She gave everything away but her books
and long white bun that swept all the stray hair
away from her eyes so she could stay grounded
in the breath of this one day.

She forgot how to push buttons
and hummed many a tune.
She laughed aloud when a frog jumped from
the shadows of her watering can
and squealed when a long snake
slithered beneath the cedar deck.

She planted more trees and designed views
from her windows that would charm her
as the winters came and the springtime grew older.

She planted with gel-nailed hands and learned
to work with body aches that demanded attention,
reworking how to bend and stand
next to weeds and wild violets.
She decided that they really held the land in place;
so, she let them be.

She was ready for the absence of worry and deep rest.
She had stored her stories and
given away her themes of grace and peace,
hope and harmony.

And every time you call her name,
she will turn and smile from her garden beds—
for Beauty is her name.

—Donna Knutson

Gardens

Invited In

I have never had to wait in a garden to be invited in,
to feel free or alive or in love with a petal,
the fragrance of earth,
or the nod of a cloud.

Through portals of hydrangeas and
pockets of raspberry phlox,
holy highs and holy lows,
nothing keeps one out of a garden.

Every soul is invited in and every kind of
child lives for the moment when it sees
the patterns and the orchestra,
the layers and the leaves,
the Majesty that calls one in,
the language all can hear.

Messengers call out from the pines
and hospitality waves from the hollyhocks
and the hibiscus shrubs.
The moss on old trees and the slits in the trunks
all tell of the mysteries that are hidden then found,
of daring hearts who planted all these roots,
of spirits that linger round lavender stems,
and cardinals bringing memories to the mothers
and grandmothers who carry the land
in their hopes and their dreams,

in the palms of their hands,
scattering seeds,
planting the trees,
having invited generations to be welcome
and to live at home
in a garden.

—Donna Knutson

I Would Not Wish

I would not wish to be young again,
and yet my world turns younger every day.

I would not wish to be young again,
expecting everyone to read my mind
and know my needs,
hoping others could fill my desires.

No, I would not wish to be young again,
and work so hard climbing tall ladders,
painting others as visionaries and saints
before their time, piling heaviness
onto others with layers of regret
or frowns of the past and
wanting my fire to be less than theirs.

To burn out from the world and
be so tired that the mind does not know
what to grasp and what to surrender.

Now, I hold onto the Heavens,
a holy wave that seeps into thoughts,
wrinkles my skin and waters down the past,
that tempers the tantrums and tells less tales.

I hold onto less need, worry, and
follow wisdom out the back door

where the sunset seeps down about the same time
in a season of sanctuary, establishing worth,
and creating contentment.

Now, I celebrate life as less accidental,
while speculating that possibly
it has carried great worth,
great wonder, great hope.

—Donna Knutson

You are the Light of the World

Dangerous and full of life,
you close my eyes,
you open my eyes.

You that has always been
will always be.

You drain from me the past,
healing memories, worries and wounds.
You dissolve the wicked and bring on the grace.

You stretch life before me like a kaleidoscope.
I tip over and empty out,
repeating nothing of the day before.

You place before me the work and fashion obstacles
not for my failing but for wisdom yet to gain.

You bring messages through the trees,
through the dead,
through the waiting.

You sew sacred threads and weave visions of hope.
You bring clarity where there is No Time
and wrap eternity in a glass filled
with heaven on earth.

Never glaring or shameful,
but born for this realm,
disguises fall away as the branches are bare
and the skies deep blue.

You bring the obedience, the material form,
the sound and a wing.

You bring peace and Presence into a body
that holds the world.

—Donna Knutson

POEMS BY ATUL RANCHOD

"There is no need to run outside for better seeing...
Rather abide at the center of your being;
for the more you leave it the less you learn.
Search your heart and see...
The way to do is to be."

—Lao-Tzu

Nature

Autumnal Notes

Autumnal notes, descending darkness,
come as the crescendo of light shifts their way.

Another season, what music becomes
when leaves pick up clues as the wind plays
an orchestral ode to fall.

Summer leaves shimmer
opulent gold, streaming musicality like Vivaldi,
bold striking colors,
beauty inspiring.

Harvest bounty is here. Jubilation!
Viridian green beaming.
Summer's transitional celebration.
Cool, crisp air blending,
breathing,
freeing.

Fall's subtlety softly ripens away.
Splendor of earth's riches in full array.

—Atul Ranchod

Gather Around

Gather around. Gaze upward.
There are sculptures, skillfully crafted.
Stoic, elegant, fig tree.

Faith isn't blind, as you can see.
The seed will never meet the leaf!
My heart has led me to this discovery.

Gentle giant, gallantly gleaming.
What a passage of living history,
fortitude in awesome solitude.

We are all connected—
be it by roots, water or tender offshoots.
There's no such stage as beginner or advanced—
just life's adventure from the Source,
root to trunk,
branch to leaf,
running its course.

Am I not exactly like this fig tree
in a different form,
the same life coursing
through my veins?

How incredibly perfect it already is;
for although my time is limited,
the joy of being is limitless!

—**Atul Ranchod**

Human Flower

From Van Gogh to Rembrandt,
Thoreau to Emerson,
masters of nature's palette,
moving and stirring
the layers underlying.

Carrying out an age-old tradition,
tilling the land and reaping the wheat,
filling the celestial sky with aroma.
The arrival of morning.

From Manet to Monet,
artists forever seeking light's play.
Science, poetry and music
cultivating the endless terrain of the heart
immersed in gratitude's domain.

We are here for a short sojourn.
Each a witness to what is inconceivable
right in front of us
because we are in such a rush.
Be still, oh fragile heart.
Be still the mind, creating a rift.

From farmer to artist,
emperor to pauper,
the ultimate human experience

tied deeply to earth and sky
beyond the parameters of why.
What grandeur to admire
from existence's undeniable power,
immortality entwined
within each
human flower.

—Atul Ranchod

Petals of Gold

Petals of gold, stories unfold—
auspicious and bold.
Vibrant primary yellow and blue.
What an awesome image of gratitude.
We are no different than a sunflower
following in leisure the orb in its breeze.

Offset by protection
from exosphere to atmosphere.
A cocoon of unimaginable fragility
keeping at bay violence and hostility.
Take into account a light breeze,
the warmth of the sun,
and the perfectly calibrated gravity.
Such attention to infinitesimal detail
so that beauty in its majesty may prevail.

I feel the earth, smell the soil.
What impeccable elegance, the dirt and I.
One and separate to rejoin again.
But for now,
singing praises of the sun,
for Life, and being alive!

—Atul Ranchod

Snowflakes

Released from the clutches
of perfection and imperfection,
freed from reality and illusion,
letting go of duality and distinction,

my grasp is greater than my imagination.
So fundamental is being human,
like a bee to pollination,
we are completely wired for
beauty's transformation.

Descending ever deeper
into the source of meditation,
the place from which
all emanates in utter perfection—
witnessing without judgment.

Divine wind caresses each snowflake.
A cosmic anomaly, this chance to be!
Water's recycled symphony
playing out so gracefully.

I can be so deeply moved
whilst being still in this breath of life.
Not wanting or needing anything—
fulfilled in my being.

—Atul Ranchod

Reclamation

Freedom Song

Words and meaning—
like light and its beaming—
inseparable is life from feeling.

Balance isn't easy
nor will it ever be.
Such is the push of destiny.

Little firefly,
stars strewn on velvet black.
Hope thrives on the slightest flicker.

Breath of life pulsates and resonates,
as demise and death narrow the noose
around the neck.
Freedom song.
Flight fulfilled, the unlost found.
Relish the light, ever so slight,
enough to illuminate the night.

Dig deep into the fecund soil
beyond this mortal coil
that so many have lost to toil.

Awaken to the day's day
apart from the problems
distracting from what's really at play.

No force in nature
dare extinguish
love's flickering flame.
Fragile, delicate, vulnerable
Eternal, immortal, unquestionable.
Inseparable, internal, invincible.

Alive and well, despite the strife.
Ignite the fire! Phoenix, spread your wings!

Reclaim the sky between gravity and flight
Ride the winds with no end in sight.

The cadence of the universe
beats perfectly within you,
writing the living poetry
upon such a rich tapestry.
At last, to leave the world of words
at the threshold and feel the grandeur
when the Divine has swallowed you whole.
Words having served their purpose,
threshold crossed, a final service—
Divine dance, unfolding verse.

—Atul Ranchod

From the Tumultuous Seas

From the tumultuous seas,
storms and thunderous waves
to the depths of the ocean.
We are this blessing of blessings
bequeathed a sail and a boat
to chart the uncharted with real hope.

How can we ever lose sight
of an inextinguishable light
that is our birthright?
Today to accept wholeheartedly
both the immortal and mortality
encased so perfectly in this human body!

—Atul Ranchod

Reclaim Our Humanity

Hope in a time of utter madness,
not to lose sight despite the sadness.

Nerves are raw and pain is
breaking the last straw.
Racism and hatred,
fires burning out of control.
Where to turn?

The red flower beats
in this garden of change.
It's time to rearrange.
If in the course of a day
we cannot take ten seconds
of beauty in any way, then
why be surprised at the outcome
and the ugliness now on
outrageous display?

At the core of the problem
we don't yet view each other
as simply human.
With strong gentleness,
with calm conviction,
seeing through the pain.
It is time to consciously plant
different seeds and reclaim

our humanity once again,
whereby gratitude
can flourish and lead us
out of our madness
and back into balance.

Now is the time to be.
Making peace our real victory.
For we are all part of the human race
by the most benevolent grace.

—**Atul Ranchod**

I Am

I wasn't nor will I be.
What an enormous incongruity!

Immersed in being,
questions melt away.
Presence fills the sails.
The dream is seen.
Reality gleams the greatest answer.
At last, it is revealed.
I am!
How powerful and simple.

To take refuge amongst the carnage.
To find peace amidst the madness.
To know without any doubt
the feeling of life
as it lives me out.
I've come home.
All I am is in this breath.
The impossible occurring in such
royal fashion.
A divine accompaniment.
From each opening and closing
of the awakened dream,
the courage needed is
to break the molds created.

We are the caretakers
of a gift unprecedented.
The dream came true
upon our first inhale.

Will we dare to awaken
from this worldly spell?

I wasn't nor will I be.
But right now,
undeniably,
I am!

—Atul Ranchod

Light
and
Dark

Into the Longest Night

Into the longest night of the year
in full fiery display happening here!

Passage of the sun
not to be taken for granted by anyone.

Relish this life
with all its idiosyncrasies.
It is the ultimate lottery.

From the Sistine to the pristine,
from pains unimaginable to joy unfathomable.

Akin to the setting sun,
each moment has only just begun.

To hold a child's enthusiasm,
a soul in constant adulation,
to be immersed in appreciation!

Then the turning towards the light
with all your heart and might.
What greater delight?

—Atul Ranchod

Light the Light

With madness and vile vicissitudes,
rampant in ignorance and carnage.
Vast layers of society enduring
chaos and upheaval.
Lighting the fire, kindling its flame,
most emphatically not giving in.
These times are pushing the envelope
of finding new strength and hope.

Incumbent on each of us
is to break free from the shackles
of concepts and ideologies that
no longer serve our inner awakening.

What good is it to have consciousness
without realizing its potential
into a genuine fruition?
We are far greater than what we've been
duped into believing!
Sentient souls that the Divine itself
chose to reside in.
There's no greater fear or relief than to begin.
If not now by you and me,
who will shift the tides of insanity?
Let's light the Light with all our might
and dispel the ignorance raging inside.

—Atul Ranchod

Palpable Darkness

Darkness has an inevitable energy.
Feared, angered, bewildered.
It lives and breathes
in the recesses in various degrees.
I faced it head on ... to see.

Grateful for its lessons.
Yes, I ran, but now I take a stand.
How palpable and potent the darkness.
Illumination descends into the caverns
of demons and disparity lurking for a lifetime.
Paralysis then analysis.
Reason's opacity, heart's tenacity.

Breeding grounds.
Conflict abounds—
then a sentient soul set free.

A carefree match—
instantly like a birthing star,
shatters and purges the weighted black.
Light in counterpoint.
The opus begins a maturation
synthesizing the two.
No longer ashamed or blamed.
Fully integrated.
Never to be the same.

—Atul Ranchod

Inner Work

Not an Easy Process

It's not an easy process
by any stretch of the imagination
to confront the intensity,
rawness and power
of the wide range of emotionality.
Immersing and allowing
the transformation to occur,
knowing the word is
where I'm called to be.

Poetry, form, structure, passion—
illusive mystery.
After some time, it is writing me.
I descend into the abyss
where I feel the massive shell
of solitude and aloneness.

This experience of connection
to the voice stirs deep within.
It is a gift and at times
difficult to bear—
a feeling so subtle and powerful.

I know not where this road will lead.
But to beauty I am forever indebted—
for it is the seed
that germinates into flowering.

Out of the greatest need I
give voice to the ineffable—
because I have felt it
by a grace beyond my reasoning.

My yearning for freedom
has led me on a most amazing journey
back home to where I truly belong.
With great conviction and care
I choose to dare
to allow the swan to fly
and feel life in all its forms.

Before I return to the elements
from where I came,
I merge with the Divine within—
the reason why I came.

—Atul Ranchod

Human Time

Human time converges
on a focal point.
Can the surgical precision
be mastered to full attention?

Like a laser dancing
on a razor's edge,
hone in the entirety
of your being.

Make the voyage from time's grasp
to know the timeless space.
Peer then, deep into the mirror.

See beyond the image reflected.
This wind and focus
can finally be connected.

There is more to human time
beyond circle and line.
Take the challenge,
and you will know the Divine.

—Atul Ranchod

Ugly Work

Addiction, resentments,
anger, frustrations.
Pain inflicted in variations.

Anesthetized, numbed,
no hope in sight.
The ugliness inside is the plight.

Safe haven in opening old wounds.
Healing can be traumatic.
Excavating to the core,
embracing without shame,
everything that I bore.

Dissolving into uncharted seas,
allowing the feeling of being at ease.
Ugly work is necessary to transmute
all that isn't me.

Today, I break generational trauma,
cultural blocks, and outdated ideas.
I do the ugly work with faith and resolve—
hope's inexhaustible light to evolve.

Face the ugliness in all its rawness,
and beauty will become clear.
Such is the nature of this human journey.

—Atul Ranchod

Gratitude

Do You Realize

Do you realize what a gift it is
to choose God every day?
Not because you have to or want to—
but because you love to.

Nothing else has the sticking power.
Hence, God is love—
not from above
but emanating from within.

Without gratification
there can be no gratitude.
Amidst the solitude,
deep into your own heart's infinite wisdom,

the connection to the Divine,
to experience the beauty
of this living time is
the opportunity given and taken.

No power on earth can shake
such a conviction.
This is no ordinary connection.
It is God in action!

—Atul Ranchod

Victim to Victor

Am I a victim?
Am I insignificant?
Am I nothing more
than a blip on this earth?

Who is the I inferring this?
Who has ever questioned
the incessant voice in the head?
Who hasn't been infected by its madness?

Silence as a counterpoint—
not mere absence, but a palpable presence.
Sinking into its musicality.
Dance of the spheres.

Shifting longstanding victimization.
Blaming, judgements, beliefs, and formulas.
Can you think about breath powering
trillions of cells with life and movement?

Has space been carved carefully enough
to sculpt gratitude into a space
of such eloquent silence—to which
nothing can ever be comparable?

Victim to victor.
Insignificant to housing

the Divine in a living residence.
Sheer unadulterated joy to be alive!

Yes, we have always held the key.
Turning it cannot be done out of fear.
This we've known all too well, for far too long,
but with great reverence and volition.

There is a power far greater at the heart
of the matter. Do we dare to summon it?
In this one life, don't you want the best of it
whilst the capacity and drive are within reach?

Innumerable elements coalescing
into this orchestrated moment.
Feel the symphony of silence
and know in your marrow, you belong!

—Atul Ranchod

Silence

Morning's Quietude

Morning has a quietude
of such profound magnitude
within the universe of solitude.

Wrapped in a blanket of silence,
palpable is the presence
before the day's events beckon.

What a privilege to acknowledge,
respond and feel without
expectation or judgement.
Simply awareness, undiluted.

To be the recipient for what's to come today
in such a quiet and charismatic way.
Birthing deeper insight into beauty's play.

—Atul Ranchod

Two Little Breaths

Those who find
the place between
two breaths
know how precisely
the timeless has
made itself felt.

Therein lies the secret key
to unlocking life's mystery.

There is no certificate, trophy or reward.
Like getting to Carnegie Hall, it takes
practice, practice, practice!
Are we not the
most amazing design,
this mortal coil,
going from each
moment of wonderment
to discover yet another?

What a marvelous motion,
this ebb and flow
in charge of oceans!

This vessel will surely disintegrate
after a life so beauteously lived—
embracing all the pains and elations,

broken down into just the sacred space
between two little breaths.

—**Atul Ranchod**

A Loud Cry

At times it is nearly impossible
to visit the inner sanctuary.
The grip of fear and misery is too acute.
Silence can be a loud cry.

In the face of such adversity,
a prayer of surrender washes over me.
Beneath the surface tension,
the true sound of silence envelopes me.

Attention and awareness combine
as the mind slowly exits time.
The Divine sings the silence into a song,
a place so profound—where I belong.

Extracting the melody of silence
is a fine art.

—Atul Ranchod

Surrendering

Melting into merging.
Layers surely peeling,
what marvel underneath revealing.

Surrendering isn't a helpless giving in.
It's an immersion into the ocean,
fully aware and knowing.

It's so easy to lose yourself
in a world that never releases its
judgements and beliefs—
and find that sacred space
where at last
mind, body and soul
are in harmony.

Surrendering to the feeling that
a day could contain a lifetime.
No questions remaining—
only benevolence and kindness within.

Divinity embraces you and
welcomes you home to the
most natural state of being—
fully awakening to life
past the facade of strife.

—Atul Ranchod

POEMS BY MEREDITH LOWRY

*"The moment one gives a close attention to anything,
even a blade of grass, it becomes a mysterious,
awesome, indescribably magnificent world unto itself."*

—Henry Miller

Blessings

Poetry

Oh, I love poetry!
That sweet rhythm of heart feeling
saying what I wish I could find words for.

Just now, a silence slips along
where the salmon swim in cycles
of seasons celebrating
how spirit smells its way home.

Where life and death
breathe between infinite worlds
eternally,
present,
a gift.

—Meredith Lowry

Three Glorious Days

When I awoke this morning
and felt Spirit breathing through me,
I realized I had not lost You.

These many days when I could not find
my connection to You,
my heart sank into a cavernous abyss
and I have been beside myself
with bone-breaking grief and loneliness,
bereft, with hopelessness escorting despair
as my only companions.

For to lose what I have waited for my entire life,
after being so close with you each moment
of those three glorious days,
I thought I would rather die
than feel such anguish.

For when held in your Sacred embrace,
my lips, eyes, heart, limbs, and soul are yours,
my roots in earth,
my mind at rest,
my soul belonging,
my spirit home—

where all things are possible
and even death cannot go.

—Meredith Lowry

Becoming

All I Truly Want

All I truly want is to feel the aliveness
and jubilance of a tender bud as it swells
in the warmth of Spring's lengthening light.

To bear joyfully the contracting forces a plant must feel
as her leaves diminish in size
toward the flowering point,
where she pauses outwardly to await
herself turning inside out.

Here, as fecundity emerges and grows,
she blushes with such intensity
of saturated color that no longer can this
new life be hidden within this delicate dancer's heart.

As her sepals slightly separate, a sliver of vermillion
shines from between her chartreuse enclosure.
And as she slowly spirals open in the
glistening newness of the virginal dew,
her pristine, tissue poppy petals gently unfold
and outstretch, as do palms upturned in holy praise.

She pauses, to fully Be in the presence of This
that she has longed for her entire life.
To be here for this momentary monumental meeting,
she brings all she has ever been
and who she is now as all she owns,

and lays herself wide open
on this transcendent altar of her ephemeral existence,
as the one glorious gift she has to give of herself.

Here for the glory of God,
she gives all she is to her Beloved,
who, in the most tenderly passionate
and light-filled embrace,
meets her where One is fully knowing
and being known.

Within such unspeakable warmth,
potency and love,
in this blazing spark,
I become filled with emptiness.

Who I have ever thought I was,
or believed myself to be,
dissolves as the sweetness of living
dies and becomes nectar
just this once.

—Meredith Lowry

Sensing My Way

Stepping onto the tightrope,
leaving this world for another,
I find myself sensing with my entire being
how to be upright for the very first time,
to stay on the line,
put one foot in front of the next.

I have to keep moving,
swaying one way then the other,
as though weaving together sides of myself
that don't often converse,
let alone walk together.

Today, for but a fleeting moment,
this line connects the steps of my life
into a dynamic balance,
the stillpoint, the hair's breadth,
a turning point in my soul.
Here I can stand free, buoyant,
held in the embrace of this Mystery,
yet one that rivets my being here in this world.

There is no security in holding onto anything,
no sure place to always stand,
no time that waits,
for all evolves with each moment's movement—
as within the pure potential of the chrysalis

where life begets itself,
through a virginal alchemy of paradoxes
between light and dark,
gravity and levity,
with each step along the line.

—Meredith Lowry

Longing and Belonging

This Unknown Road

Here on this unknown road,
the silence, thick as night,
is coming from great expanses
to find you.

Where are you now?
With no lamp or key,
with only the faint melody of time
beckoning,
as it flows from the horizon
where all find their true home.
A place of rest.

Is it my time?
Can one really be taken back
to such freshness
after coming so far?

Go no farther.
Let your breath sink into that deep dark ocean
where you are breathed
by the stars' becoming.

There is a precious pearl
in one of those craggy oysters
in the thick muck at the bottom of the sea,
where life emerges inside the quiet deep stillness–

waiting, growing, ripening.

What would it take
for you to open your shell just enough
that your softest, most vulnerable self
could let the Ocean in
to bathe and so gently move you
with its eternally present Tide?

What do you most deeply long for in
your heart of hearts?

—Meredith Lowry

Grandma's House

I sit here this steamy summer morning
in my grandmother's house,
where my soul has always lived and bathed
in a love so tender, so sweet;
an unconditional connection,
as timeless as the sun's presence
throughout the nights and days of my life,
warming as the crimson becoming vermillion,
turning yellow light of this August sunrise.

And at other times with the crisp, sparkling, twinkling
presence of the stars on a January night,
when reflections of the stillness of sky and lake
merge without a seeming boundary between,
their breathing soothes and
illuminates such a deep space in myself
where beauty, peace and joy arise,
with the grace of a far-reaching breadth of a rising tide.

Seamlessly and silently swimming its way
up towards the river's source,
rising and falling,
with the same breath breathing
along to where the inwardly known home beckons—
calling out to each one,
shad, salmon, or soul,
whether now or before the dammings,

promising repose after life's long, full and
arduous journey upstream.

Now as I lie on my bed
I sense the coming and going of my breath,
the rising and falling, filling and emptying,
subtly sinking into a shallower slowing synchrony,
where breathing becomes
Life's breath breathing me,
and through each guiding our way home.

As the sun appears to set in the west,
I find my own rest in my grandmother's house
amidst these rolling hills by the
flowing Susquehanna
where the post office would say
I have never lived,
yet where life and love has woven
a timeless spacious home ever with me,
even now,
wherever I go.

—Meredith Lowry

Presence

Sunrise at Canyon de Chelly

Look overhead—
the stars are beginning to hide the stuff they are made of
as the blue yawn of night delivers us
from sleep once again.
Before the earth's first breath speaks
its warm whisper of golden light
upon this canyon mother's red rock rugae,
it glistens, where the river of life has bore
a myriad of stories
written upon wailing walls,
bearing witness to what we most fear
and love.

Now that the light sinks into the canyon,
warm breath becomes wild winds
which move through these valleys
and caves of joys and sorrows
like nomads who, for generations,
tended their sheep as ten thousand tears
dried into salt.

In the freshness of this morning,
I am watched over by cavernous sandstone eyes–
sometimes seeing,
yet always beholding
how redemption will come if one waits long enough,
and by whom the web of why is being woven.

For it is a testament of devotion,
these handholds carved with such care
along Yebuchei trail,
these juniper berries dried and beaded
as blessings and passed on,
these ochre drawings and stories of the old ways.

And when I hear tender hearts
speaking into thin air
of courageously forgiving
what never should have been,
something mysterious arises
as a stillness calms the wind
and a silent murmuring in the river
seems to whisper:

all is well, all is well.

—Meredith Lowry

The Secret Fire

Let us be what we are in the heart of things,
the Fire, the Loving Presence,
the Listening, the Courage,
the warmth we can always come home to.

When the dawn breaks and the first whispers fly
over the horizon, bringing secrets on
wings of warm breath
through our hair, over our skin,
into each cell of light that shimmers in joy,
in greeting, in love, in praise, in communion,
we need not hide any longer.

The secret is being told
with each breath being written upon
each transparent surface,
each translucent membrane,
each opening to what we are,
who we truly are,
what brings us life,

and how this Eternal fire can ripen
the fruits of our soul's longing.

—Meredith Lowry

Renewal

The Summoning

Walking in the woods that year,
I lived too much inside myself,
gazing at the horizon and moon,
watching the clouds play along the edges and ridges
before the rains came.

Not yet being called by name, I waited.

Today is the day I was summoned
from my long winter,
into the forest grove where a rocky patchwork path
led me to an ancient gnarly stump,
moist with a mane of verdant moss.

I found myself drawn to a soft plush tuft
where I could nestle
near the old man's beard,
having grown for its lifetime.
From tips of silver twigs swelling with growing life,
the breezes filled me with songs of chickadees
and I could hear the fox sparrow call
my name into the sky with great delight.

Here, finally, a deep winter weariness
clinging fervently to its last breath–

curled up, dried, then dropped,
as the pin oak's last trembling leaf does,
before all is given over
to Spring's newness.

—Meredith Lowry

Deepest Darkness

In this deepest darkness,
may an illuminating
Ancient Star Light
blossom within
the labyrinth of our hearts.

As only children can imagine,
bending their bodies
along the arc of light,
inscribing magical blessings
upon the horizon,
making the ordinary sacred—

So the world can always
begin anew.

—Meredith Lowry

POEMS BY GERSHON MITCHEL

(a.k.a. Kaptain Dignity the Expounder)

*"If with only a drop of poetry or love
we could placate the anger of the world,
but that can only be done by a
striving and resolute heart."*

—Pablo Neruda

Dignity

Just Imagine

I don't know if God is more real than
the man in the moon.
I do know human dignity.

Dignity is the foundation and
driving force that underpins
all Human Rights.
It's the plumbline in constructing
the scaffolding for a new
sociopolitical and cultural structure—
the new North Star for recalibrating the
MORAL compass of our collective ship
and our-very-own-selves.

Human dignity does not require
creating something that didn't exist before.
It is an organic, reflexive impulse
born into the human family.

People of faith celebrate
human dignity as a gift from God.

I do not know agape love or
spiritual enlightenment or
revelation or redemption.

I do know human dignity—

the lowest of our higher angles.
It is the collective call that
reinvigorates the spirit of the soul,
the abstract concept
that brings the human spirit
down to earth through the capacity
to exercise our free will.

How do we conduct ourselves
given our circumstances?
Do we honor this,
ignore it or
violate this impulse?

Dignity cannot co-exist with
power or dominance or
honor or rank.

It is not some empty, hollow
platitude uttered from the mouths of
self-serving politicians or
corporate media talking heads.

It is baked into our DNA
and empowers us to find
worth and value in
our own eyes,
no more or less than
the rest of all sentient beings.

Once recognized and acknowledged,
your stance in the world—

to life,
to your relations,
to yourself,
to others,
to Mother Nature—
becomes altered in the
most positive and

respectful manner.
What a beautiful, harmonious
world this would be,
with folks' and kinfolks' dignity.
Just imagine.

—Gershon Mitchel

They Are Like Kisses

A teacher without students
is like a character without an author,
a rose without its perfumed fragrance.

Just as one cannot argue someone into
liking the taste of a beer,
the same is true of love,
friendship and new ideas.

They are like kisses
and go by favor.

We say and we say and we say—
we promise, we engage and declare'
til a year from tomorrow is
yesterday and yesterday
is where?

One has got to be aware
of something before
claiming it
as their own—
and claiming something is not
the same as sustaining it.

—Gershon Mitchel

Preparing the Ground

Like it or not,
we are a species of
moral beings imbued with
an intuitive, reflexive impulse of
inherent human dignity.

Who hasn't felt the
sharp sting of humiliation?
You don't have to ponder this feeling,
for it is physical and visceral.
You know when your human dignity
Has just been violated!

The best teachers know that
the best seeds will not root in hard,
dry, cracked-clay soil.
The ground needs preparation
to receive them.

The loam of human dignity
is the great fertilizer.

It's what makes humanity humane,
where we all recognize and acknowledge
the others' capacity to be moral, as well.

We all possess a sense
of absolute inner worth and
command respect for ourselves
as rational beings in the world.

We activate our common
inherent human dignity as
the moral imperative
that bridges every breach.

—Gershon Mitchel

The Light of a Kindled and Open Heart

A human rights-based value system approach
to learning and thinking has the potential
to present another way that strikes
a deeper chord— one that
pricks the conscience,
stirs the blood
and elevates those
who have an unmediated tendency
to make people better
by toughing their moral fiber.

All that we are is the result of what
we have thought and imagined.
For better or worse,
the world is comprised of
our thoughts and imaginings.

A human rights-based value systems
s its upon and is the driving force
that sends the spirit earthward
with added respect for the intrinsic worth
of every individual and species that
the planet sustains through her
life-affirming biosphere.

A human rights-based value system
of dignity to learning is an idea

that can strike the intellect
as an exceptional presentation of
an important truth.

Let it be judged and measured by
the frame of mind it induces.

While understanding that the utterances of
the noblest truth cannot be read without the
light of a kindled and open heart,
the idea of a simple spark is predicated upon
both a smooth and a rough stone surface
striking each other.
No spark,
no fire,
no energy.

The people are the smooth surface,
the teacher is the rough.

If the intellect is the handmaiden
to the conscience,
and a shift in consciousness is
what is called for in these dark and
foreboding times, then that which informs
the intellect is of vital consequence.

A dignity-centric value system
can trigger a channel for the
re-enchantment of the human spirit,
one that holds the promise of
a more compassionate humanity.

A force that can stir the vast wealth
of human potential to
positively affect the future,
heal the wounded,
realign souls,
make the world less ugly
and draw us together in the
communion of our common labor.

—Gershon Mitchel

A Tender-Minded Temperament

To do the right thing is usually never easy.
To do the easy thing is not always right.
To do the right thing is usually never popular.
To do the popular thing is not always right.

To do the right thing when no one is looking
is one thing.
Some call this integrity.
To do the right thing when all eyes are upon you
is another thing,
Some call this courage.

While integrity mitigates corruption,
without courage, wisdom will not bear fruit.

As men think, so they go.
As men go, so nations go.

"Empire thinking" begets empire,
and "market-value" thinking begets
a culture and society driven by values of
profit, greed, gain, competition— which,
in turn, spawns a tough-minded temperament
that stiffens and freezes the heart.
Over time, the heart becomes
encrusted with callous indifference.

A dignity-based, human rights value system
of thinking begets a culture and society
driven by an ethos of morals;
dignity, worth and equality—
which, in turn, spawns a tender-minded
temperament and compassionate motivations.

If this is not on the radar of the imagination
of the general public, then what?

—Gershon Mitchel

Mindfulness as a Meaningful Exercise

In our current zeitgeist,
the concept of mindfulness is popular
as one solution to address the
current wave of
violence and hate.

This is good and I
would to proffer a suggestion:
Mindfulness refers to what is
happening in our interior selves—
thoughts, feelings, emotions.

When practicing it, I invite you
to focus on your
inherent human dignity and
what it's telling you.

This will show you
what is right or wrong,
good or bad.
It presents you with
your own barometer
to explore and examine
not only your actions but
if your thoughts comport to
your own standards.

More than a social
tool for self-examination,
it will give you gauge on current events—
not only in the world at large,
but in your personal reality.

Your inherent human dignity
should empower, ground, and anchor you,
allowing you to shape and form
your individual character
and own social norm, if you will.

It presents you with an opportunity
to exercise your free will, for no one
should be compelled to think or
act this way or that.

The mindfulness of human dignity
is a meaningful exercise to engage with.
But first—
It presupposes that you deem
human dignity worthy of
cogitating upon!

—Gershon Mitchel

First Things First

They came like rolling thunder
and crashing symbols,
pounding Japanese Taiko drums
atop the crests
of fierce and furious waves
upon the ocean seas.

Wild horses, white stallions,
pink nostrils flared,
great manes flowing,
tails swishing this way and that,
riding astride six winged angels
holding banners aloft
with flaming letters that read:

More dignity, less humiliation.
More dignity, less domination.
More dignity, less shame.
More dignity, less hate.

Throngs of we-the-people lined the shore
as far as one could see.
The wild horses kept thundering on.
Waiting, waiting, waiting—
no one stirred a whit
to what was before them,
hidden in plain sight—

a black swan!

It was the anointed time and day.
The stars and constellations aligned.
The Mayan, Inca and Aztec
ancient calendars marked.
The Hindu Vedas and Kabbalists,
Sufis and spiritual wisdom teachers
all coinciding to this day—
a revelation of a universal truth.

Thundering wild horses kept coming—
glistening black, dappled gray, chestnut brown,
palominos and painted pintos.
Four more winged angels arrived
with black banners and
flaming letters reading:

More dignity, less rudeness.
More dignity, less indifference.
More dignity, less dismissal and diminishing.
More dignity, less ridicule and belittling.
More dignity, less contempt and disdain.
More dignity, less bullying and coercion.

We-the-people on the shore wielded
binoculars, spy glasses, and telescopes—
still not a hint of recognition
as the wild horses kept coming
along with three winged angels
carrying banners:

More dignity, less mocking and scoffing.
More dignity, less trickery and manipulation.
More dignity, less suspicion and vilification.
More dignity, less exploitation and exclusion.
More dignity, less revulsion and depravity.

What/who were they/we-the-people waiting for?
Saints and prophets.
The Messiah.
Jesus or Buddha or Mohammad.
Popes and kings.

King Arthur and his knights.
Robin Hood and his merry band.
Cisco and Poncho, the Lone Ranger and Tonto.
Quixote and Sancho!
Maybe a giant, one-eyed Cyclopes or
Mother Mary or alien ships
rising from the oceans' depths
peopled with Hindu gods and goddesses
in the company of their Greek and Roman namesakes.
Maybe Mother Nature herself!

The apparitions began to reach the shoreline
and thread themselves
in and around and through
the teeming throng of we-the-people.

Spirit shadows were accompanied by
beauteous siren music from the heavenly spheres.
As the sun sunk into the ocean,
the crescent moon began to peek above the cliffs,

the phantasms beginning to fade,
one last banner read:

More words, less munitions.

The sun sank deeper, its rays pouring forth.
We-the-people turned *our* backs,
hung *our* heads . . . and departed.

None saw the final banner
trailing across the ocean
above the cliffs, beneath the stars,
words aflame:

Would you recognize me,
The Truth,
if I came in a guise
other than what you imagined
or expected in your mind's eye?

Nary a soul turned back
to steal a final glance.
Many pillars of salt were
later found.

A profound betrayal,
the tragedy that is humankind.

Beyond words, beyond tears!

If only we-the-people
made the time—
cared enough to bother—

and see
with reason from the heart
and the imagination of the mind.
First things first.

—Gershon Mitchel

About the Poets

MEET OUR POET, GINA MAZZA:

Gina has been living her passion as a word provocateur and creative alchemist for more than three decades. She is the author of three books in the personal growth category, including *Everything Matters, Nothing Matters*, which was praised in *Publisher's Weekly*.

As an independent journalist/features correspondent, Gina's byline can be spotted in media outlets around the world. She has profiled a diversity of thought leaders—physicians, PhDs, research scientists, theologians, politicians, mythologists, conscious evolutionists, CEOs, pro athletes, change agents, best-selling authors and a few celebs—as well as everyday people of extraordinary faith who do good works and help us envision a beautiful future.

In her core work as a writing coach, creative muse, book editor, communications professional and publishing consultant, Gina has helped hundreds of individuals refine their writing projects and send them off into the world. Her clients have gone onto secure literary agents, land book/film deals, build successful brands and enjoy exciting literary careers. Gina also has a solid background in entrepreneurship, PR, corporate marketing, event planning, and the use of intuitive guidance to elucidate one's work, mission and soul purpose. She graduated cum laude from Florida State University and has taught as an adjunct lecturer in creative writing at several universities.

One of Gina's main fascinations—in her work and in general—is dissecting life's mysteries to expose its grandeur. Her inward path has led her around the world—including Italy, England, France, Ireland, Chile, Patagonia, Bosnia, Canada and across the United States—exploring and working within intentional and eco-communities, sacred sites and creative incubators with others in the realms of quantum storytelling, the healing arts and ancient wisdom traditions.

As a trained intuitionist, Gina's connection to Creator and creation energy is finely attuned. For her, one of the best things in life is communing with the Holy Muse, luring ever closer to it through incisive words, verse and discourse. Her poetry contained within these pages offers a taste of this expressed God-locution.

Gina lives near Nashville, Tennessee, surrounded by wildly talented musical / creative writers and artists. She is the proud mama of her adult daughter and son, and Gigi (like a grandmother, only cooler) to her grandson. Gina and her true love remain perpetually grateful that all of their cherished loved ones are thriving and living life to the fullest—giving all praise and glory to God.

ginamazza.com | ginamazza@me.com

MEET OUR POET, SCOTT A. TERRELL:

Scott Terrell is an accomplished aerospace machinist (some of his widgets are on the planet Mars), and a clairsentient empath who is extremely sensitive to energy.

Scott's journey into the headwaters of the heart of God commenced in earnest after 40 years of misery and self-inflicted suffering, including a bad car accident that broke his spine in a burst fracture. During his arduous, painful recovery, Scott slowly emerged from his dark night of the soul by immersing in a power far greater than himself. This power inspired him to write voraciously.

As words magically spilled upon the page, Scott was initially unaware of the depths that these poems would awaken within him. To this day, Scott continues to enter a state of high consciousness, where he becomes more than he is as inspired writings pour forth (while surrounded in Colorado by his two daughters and four grandchildren). It is his sincere wish that all who read his poetry feel uplifted and open to allowing the holy word into their hearts.

scottyolie28@hotmail.com

MEET OUR POET, DONNA KNUTSON:

Donna is an Ordained Interfaith Minister from One Spirit Seminary in New York City, a spiritual director who trained in the Jungian Mystical Christian Tradition at The Haden Institute in North Carolina, and a graduate of Wisdom School in San Antonio, Texas.

In 2018, she created Sanctuary County Cottage, a retreat center on acreage between Omaha and Lincoln, Nebraska, as a place for rest, private and group retreats, and coursework. She has brought her expertise in garden design (having owned a business in this field for nine years) into her retreat center, which is graced with a labyrinth, landscaped flowerbeds and enchanted wooded pathways.

Before moving to the country, Donna taught classes and led retreats at United Church of Christ in Omaha focused on the topics of grief, trauma and loss, as well as writing about beauty in the ordinary world and finding the mystic within.

A near-death experience in 2008 changed Donna's life forever. Since then, she has not stopped writing about the beauty, awe, hope, and connection to the Spirit of the Living God. She signs her poetry "Beauty Donna" as a reminder of the word she kept hearing during her NDE.

Donna is the author of *Finding God on Mayberry Street: Seasons of Spirituality on Poems and Reflections* and *Finding God on Mayberry Street: A Reflective Journal*. In search of the deeper mysteries, she has traveled to Italy and France, and walked the El Camino de Santiago in Spain. Inspired by the rising of the divine feminine, Donna believes that humanity is now awakening, and as we transform and heal our interior trauma and pain, we create portals of deeper connection to the Inner Knower.

When not gardening and writing about the Living God that lives within us, Donna adores spending time with her family.

Donnaknutson4@gmail.com

MEET OUR POET, ATUL RANCHOD:

Born in South Africa and raised in California, Atul has been intently writing poetry for a decade, much of it inspired by his love for and connection to roses and their representation of life. For him, poetry is a means of communicating life's beauty as well as examining the darkness that we all encounter as part of being human.

The strongest influence on Atul's inner world has been his relationship with Prem Rawat, a global peace ambassador, whom he has known since he was a child. Through this friendship, Atul has received the gift of Knowledge, which serves as a practical means to experience one's inner divinity. In addition to a daily meditation practice, this wisdom has provided Atul with a sense of stability in the sea of change that he has experienced throughout his life.

Moving frequently in his youth, Atul was forced to continuously adapt to new people and places, thereby unable to form lasting relationships. As an adult, Atul continued to travel extensively to India, Australia, Canada, Singapore, South America, parts of Africa, and most of Europe and the United States. His favorite locale is Florence, Italy, where he studied art for two years and hosted a one-man art show on the Gallery on the Arno River.

For the past 10 years, he has finally found peace and constancy in a small California town between Los Angeles and Santa Barbara. These days, he recites his poetry during monthly gatherings at the Universalist

Unitarian Church, and enjoys playing golf, chess and tennis. His daily road bike rides in the countryside serve as inspiration for his poetry and much of the imagery he captures in his photographs.

Atul is the author of *Top of the Water*, a collection of award-winning poems that explore nature, beauty and the divine. His former poetry blog reached people in more than 90 countries. He has a 22-year-old son who is launching his career as a pilot. Both his mother and Atul are extremely proud of him.

Baraldi007@gmail.com

MEET OUR POET, MEREDITH LOWRY:

Meredith wrote and bound her first poetry book when only six years old. In 2001, at age 46, poetry was sparked within her again as she created original pieces and learned "by heart" the works of contemporary poets. Meredith experiences poetry as conversations with the Great Mystery and an opening into other dimensions, where something behind, between and beyond the words emerges and speaks to her.

Meredith's lifelong exploration of this invisible, numinous world has included immersion into spirituality, quantum physics, medicinal botany and herbalism, archetypal and embodied psychology, and homeopathy—leading to a career as a Doctor of Osteopathy, which she has practiced for nearly 40 years. As a DO, her approach combines conventional medical skills with various holistic mind body modalities such as Biodynamic Cranial Osteopathy, classical homeopathy, anthroposophical medicine, NARM (a gentle, embodied way to release developmental trauma), and movement and gesture as metaphor.

Meredith blends her love of poetry into her practice, by often reciting or printing poems for her patients so they feel understood and companioned, or by giving specific ones to them as "prescriptions" to follow to accompany them in their healing journeys.

"This creates a space for them drop further into their own inner tempo and healing resources following a session," she comments. "I find great joy in finding just the right poem."

These days, Meredith works as a life and mind body health coach, drawing upon a combination of guided imagery, embodied practices, homeopathy, Human Design, Gene Keys, evolutionary and archetypal astrology, and gentle touch to help individuals sense into and attune more fully to their souls' intention, movement and how it informs their lives—often through learning to slow down and drop into an inner stillness as a doorway into a subtler sensing behind the physical world as we usually know it.

Meredith also finds replenishment through the stillness in nature, where she loves being and taking small groups who wish to explore an embodied connection with the natural world around them, within themselves and between one another through subtler sensing, attuning and expression.

Other than her six-year-old version of a book, this collection is the first time Meredith has shared her poems with a reading audience.

meredithlowrydo@gmail.com

MEET OUR POET, GERSHON MITCHEL:

Gershon worked an eclectic mix of jobs earlier in his life—forging steel in Pittsburgh's mills, laying railroad ties like John Henry, running machinery in the Wonder Bread factory and loading UPS tractor trailers on the midnight-to-eight-a.m. shift, often in the dead cold of the northeastern winter.

Simultaneously, he earned a B.A. and Master's degree in education, taking practicums in settings like state mental hospitals where he taught teenage boys in the juvenile court system. Upon graduation and after a circuitous, six-month road trip in a 1956 Chevy belair station wagon, Gershon ended up working as a "walk on" in the Yellowstone fires of 1988—at the time, the largest forest fire in recorded United States history. After four weeks on the fire, he ventured up through Glacier National Park, Vancouver Island and Banff, Canada, eventually dropping anchor in the San Francisco Bay area.

There he taught middle school classes for two decades in private, public, parochial, Catholic and Yeshiva, Jewish settings. During his sojourn out West, Gershon also studied intensely with the Chabad, Hasidic community and the Sonoma State University's Holocaust Studies department.

Along the way, Gershon engaged with the hippy counter culture of that time, married, had two sons, divorced and temporarily went off the rails for three days and nights—ultimately pulling himself back to the land of reality and grateful for a second chance at life.

Since retiring from teaching and now back in Pittsburgh, Gershon has found a new groove for himself through writing. He continues to strive for "hitting his stride" and singing the song he's come here to sing to humanity, after years of falling "deep in the valley of my dry-bone dreams" (quoting Bob Dylan's song, "Dignity"). This is the first time Gershon's poetry has been published in book form.

gershonmitchel@yahoo.com

Made in the USA
Middletown, DE
07 November 2023

42121481R00176